THE RETURN

Adrain Chesser in collaboration with ritualist Timothy White Eagle

Daylight

For the First People, domination of the natural world was an unknown concept. When Europeans came, their power was undeniable and their ideas of domination and God directly contradicted the First People's ideals. The European attitudes toward the indigenous world felt literally monstrous to the First People.

With the European triumph, vital aspects of the rich culture of the First People were lost. Some important threads of indigenous wisdom survived through verbal tradition, songs, stories, and rituals. A few Elders held these and passed on to new generations ancient ideas and prophecies for the future.

Now a growing number of people are looking for a harmony they find lacking in contemporary life. Many people hear a thread or two of indigenous wisdom and find it appealing. Only a few explore the ideals in depth. And fewer still consider the primal step of living in an ancient way.

The subjects in *The Return* are predominately not indigenous. Most carry European ancestry, and most come in one form or another from the disenfranchised margins of mainstream America. Most are poor, some are queer, some are transgender, some are hermits, and some are politically radical. All believe that major shifts are needed in the way modern society interacts with the natural world. These willing pioneers are stepping off into uncertain terrain, searching for something lost generations ago.

In their search, they struggle to be released from old ways of being. Cars, soda pop, cell phones, and cigarettes follow them. Convenience has a magnetic power. Addictions, cravings, and desires are hard to break. These pioneers seek a new way in the world while still learning to let go of the old. These are uncommon heroes shedding layer by layer the learned domestication of the dominator culture.

The world was once a wild garden. The First People would tell us that our human role was, and is, to tend the Garden without intrusion. To value all things in the web of life equally, remembering first that all things are related. To live and eat and love without dominion.

What these heroes seek is a physical thing: a rich, sustaining landscape and a balanced interaction with all of nature. It is a change in the human heart they seek–in their own hearts and in the hearts of the world. Equal exchange is freedom from dominion and brings with it a different kind of power–the power of balance, of giving back as much as, or more than, you take.

These new heroes are on a journey, like ancient heroes on a mythic quest, discovering that the greatest adventure is finding the way to return home. For them, home is a wild garden: an ideal, a way of life, a return to what once was. The wild garden is a place the human soul knows. Every person has ancestors who lived in that wild garden; it is a universal thing we share.

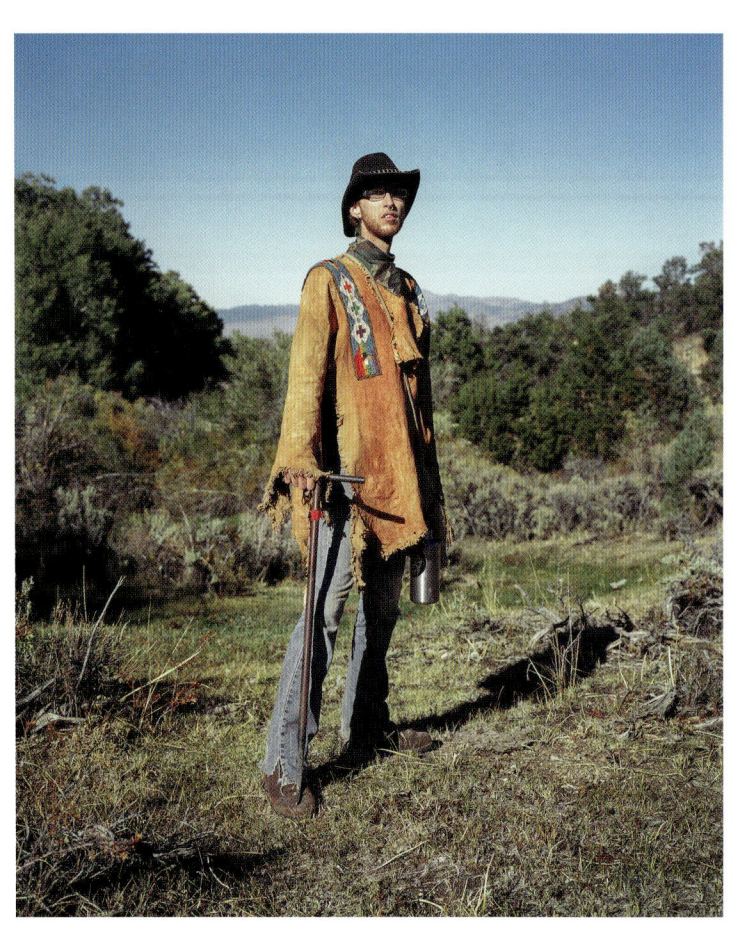

Dedicated to the memory of JP Hartsong

The world was once a wild garden.

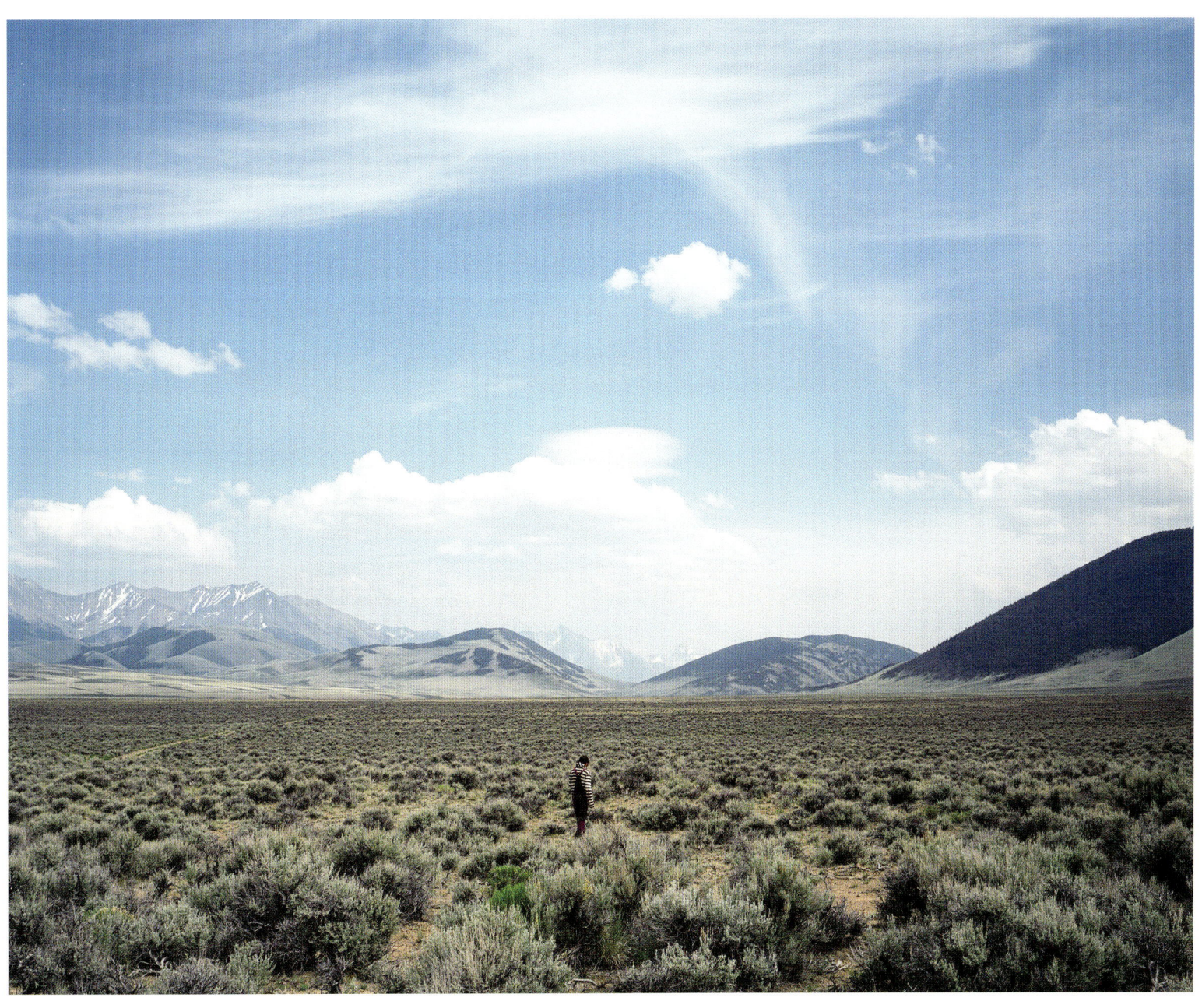

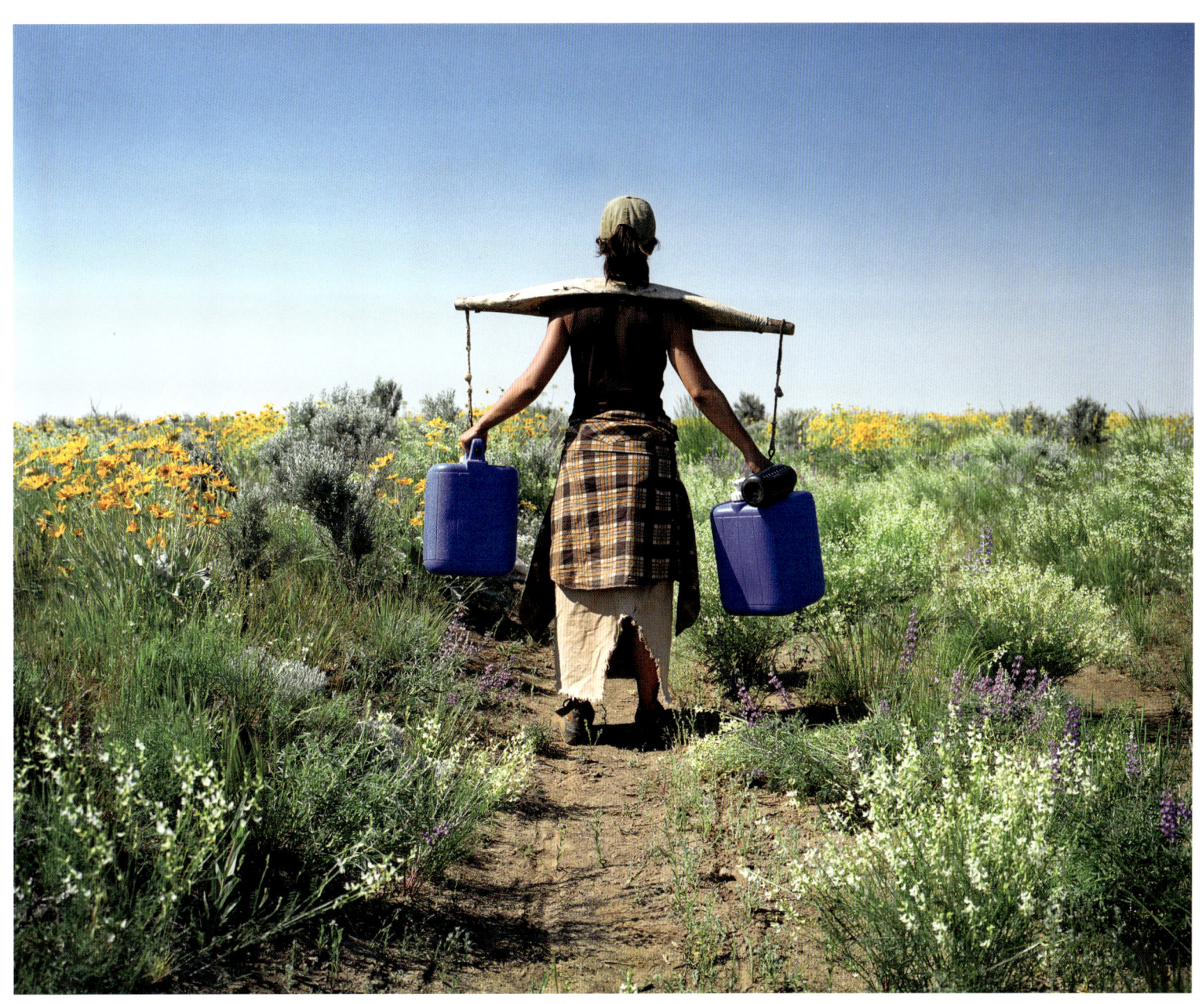

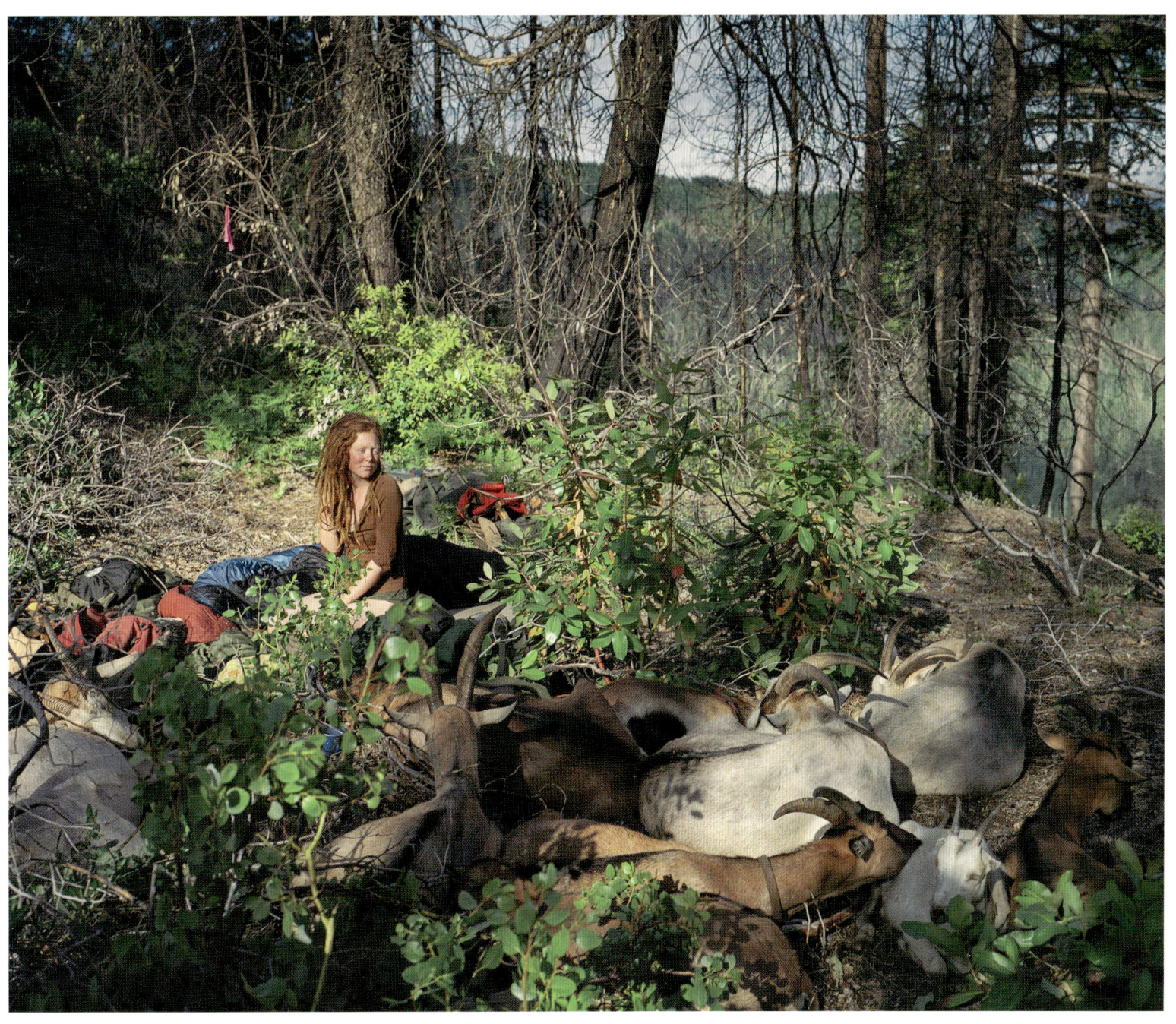

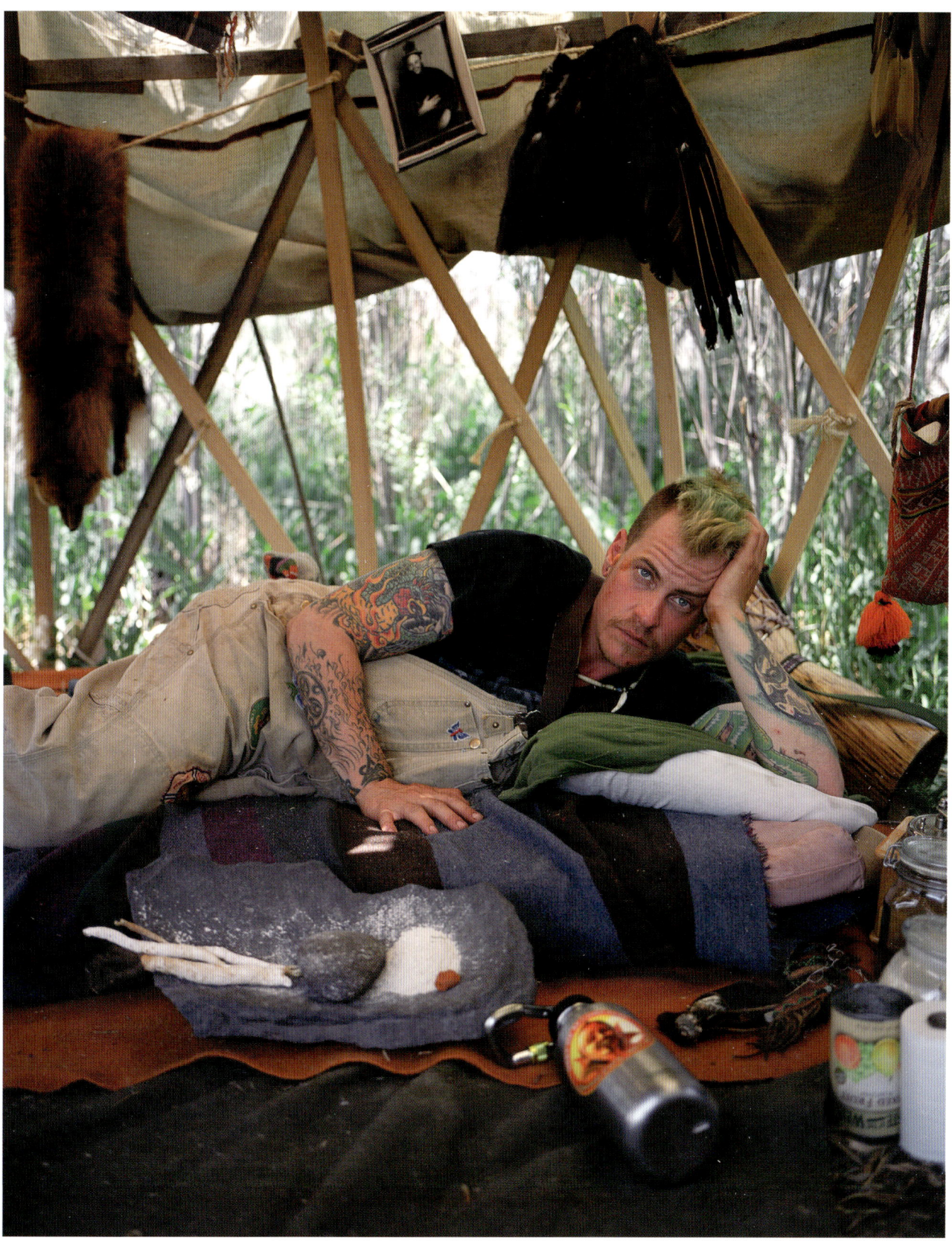

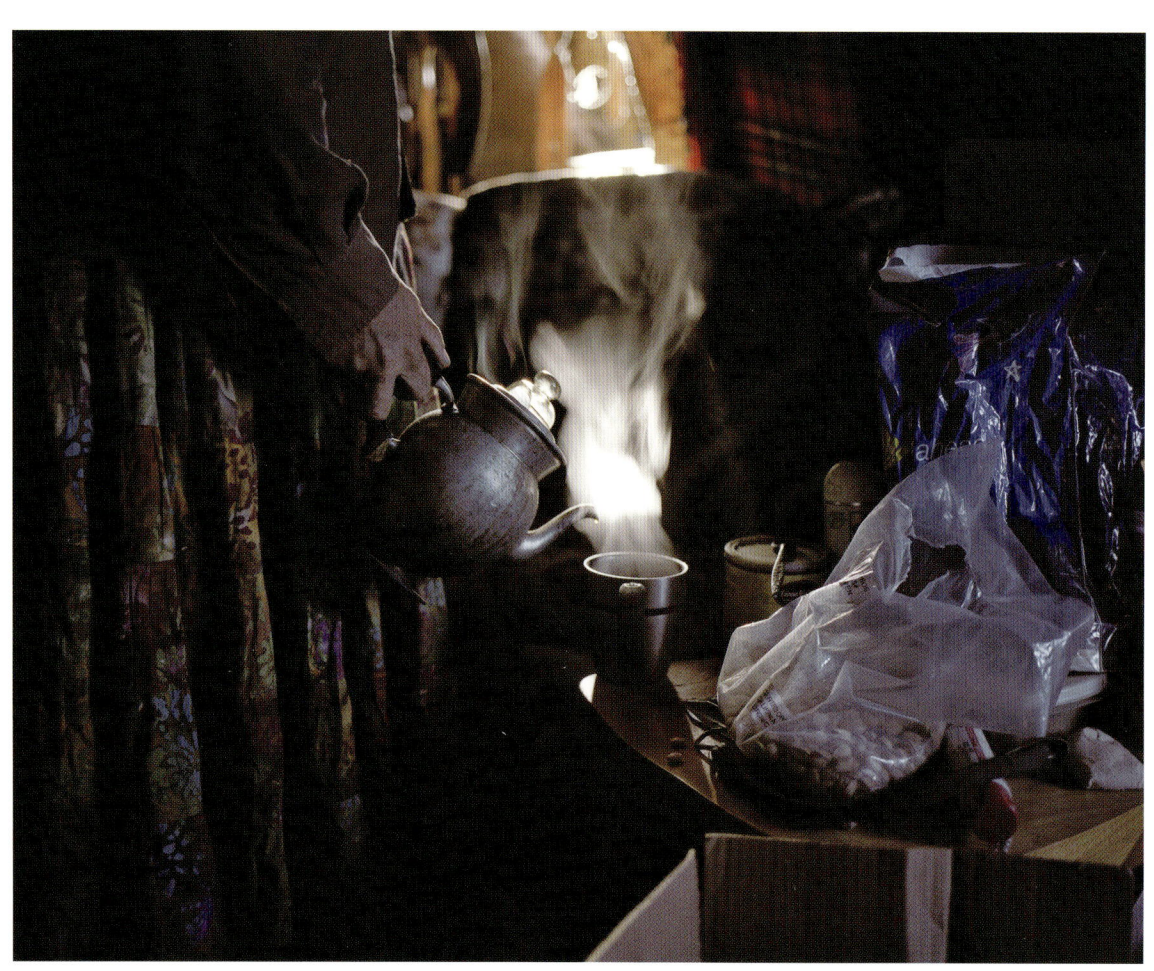

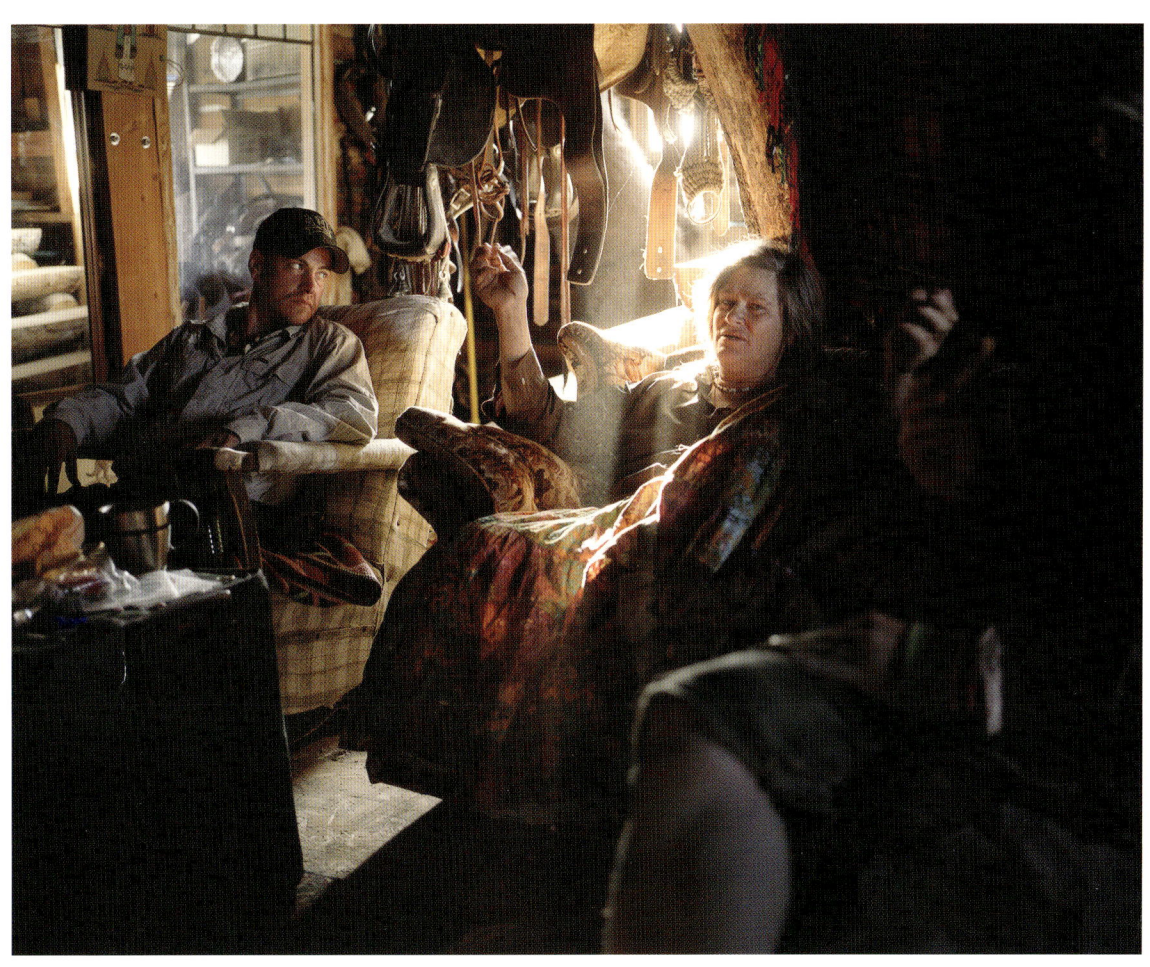

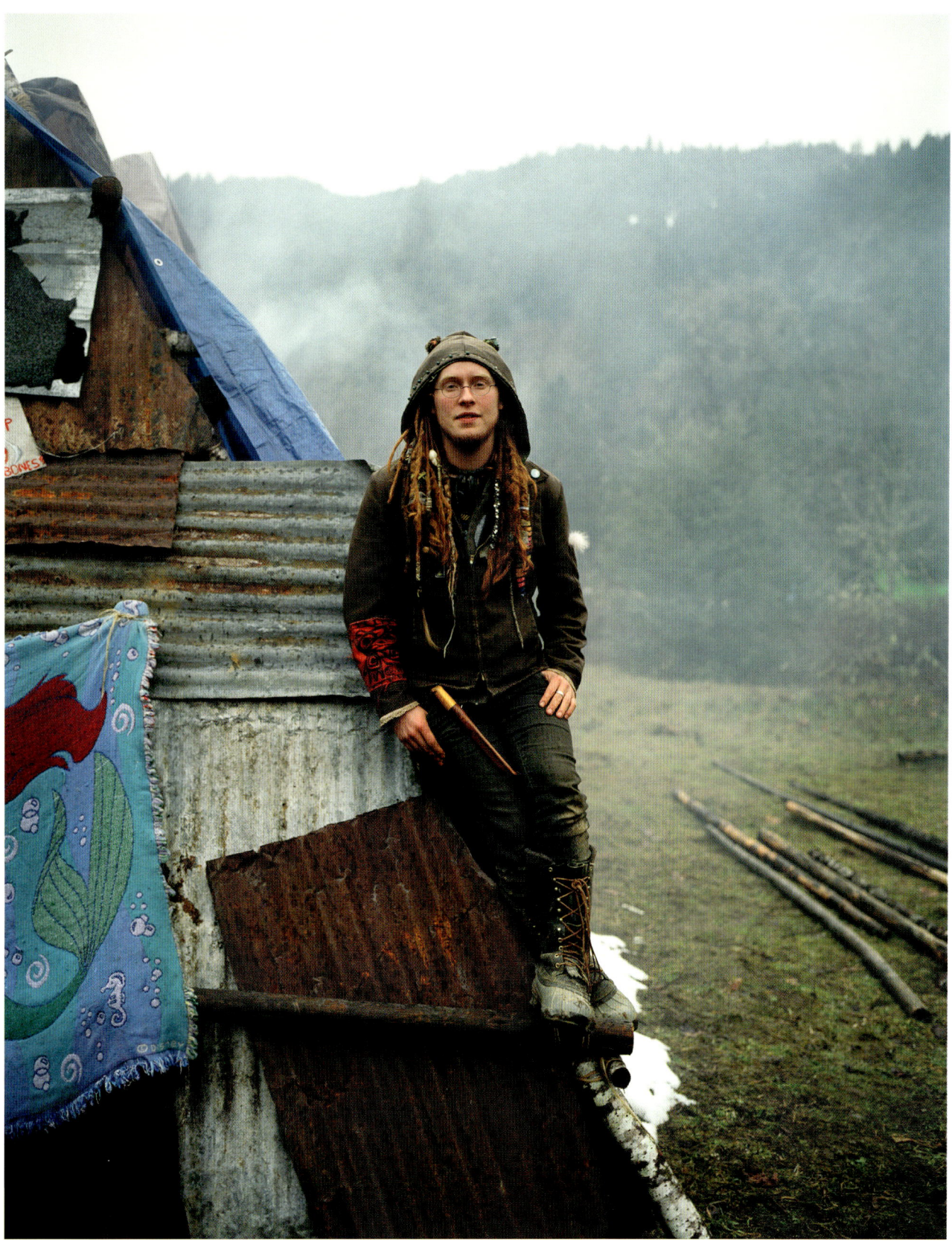

I light my wild dreams and seeds on fire inside myself
May they grow strong and cared for

I initiate myself

Seed bearer
Wild one
Earth healer
Earth speaker
Earth dreamer

May my purpose and path become clear
May I walk in strength, full of knowing
Fulfilling my purpose here
May I hold myself and others gently and with patience
May I continue to decolonize and rewild and grieve and heal
And sing and sing and sing
May I hear the calling
May I allow myself to be summoned
May I walk with strength, empowered
May I allow myself to be me
May I listen to earth's call
May I continue to hear earth's call
May I know my place in the universe
May I remember I am loved and needed and incredible
May I know and trust myself
May I feel love and support all around me
May I hold myself in so much care
May I offer myself enough rest and support
To feel able to be called into action
May I be resilient in change and challenge
And weather the storms like a wildfire

—Amara Snakeroot Hollowbones

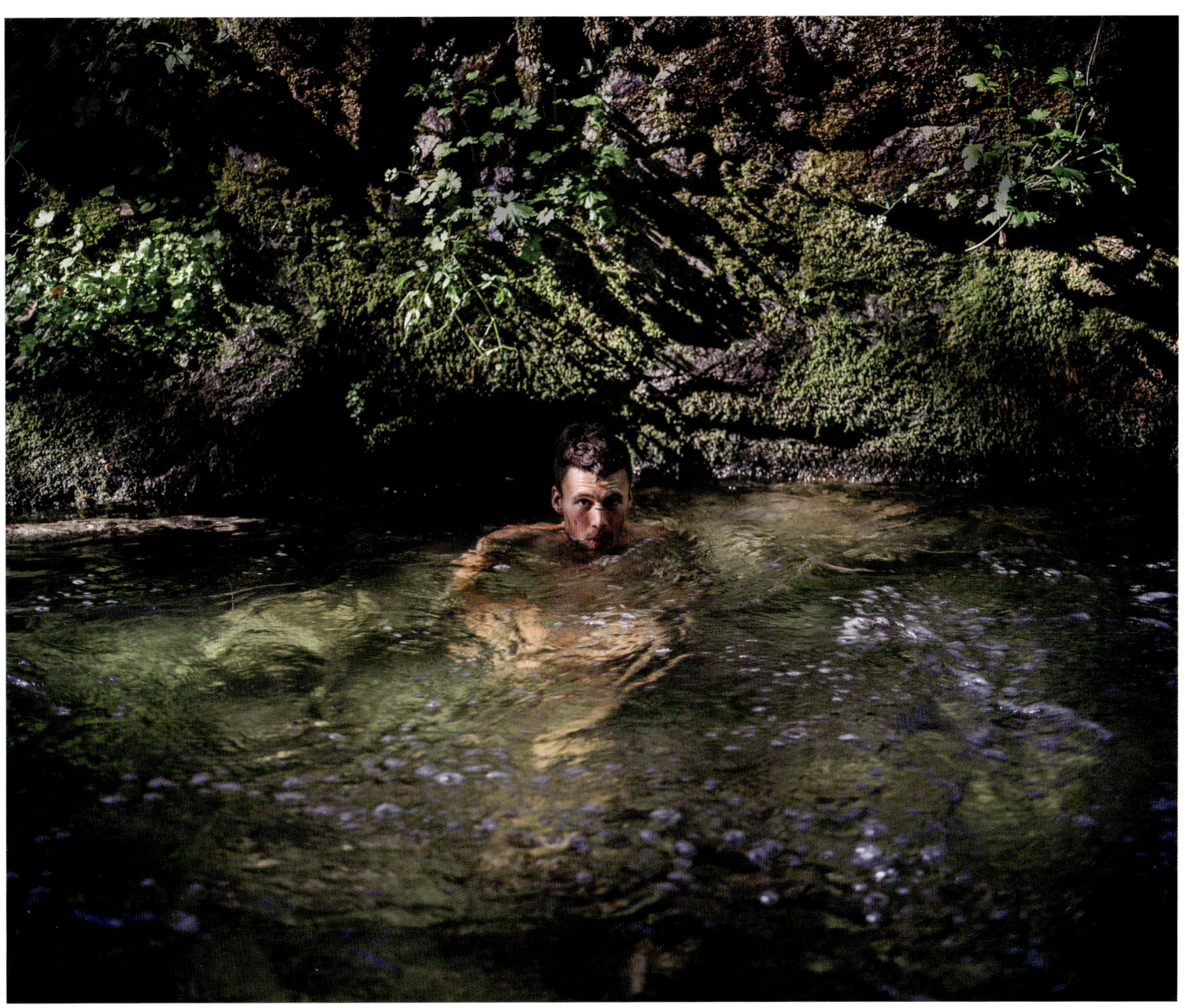

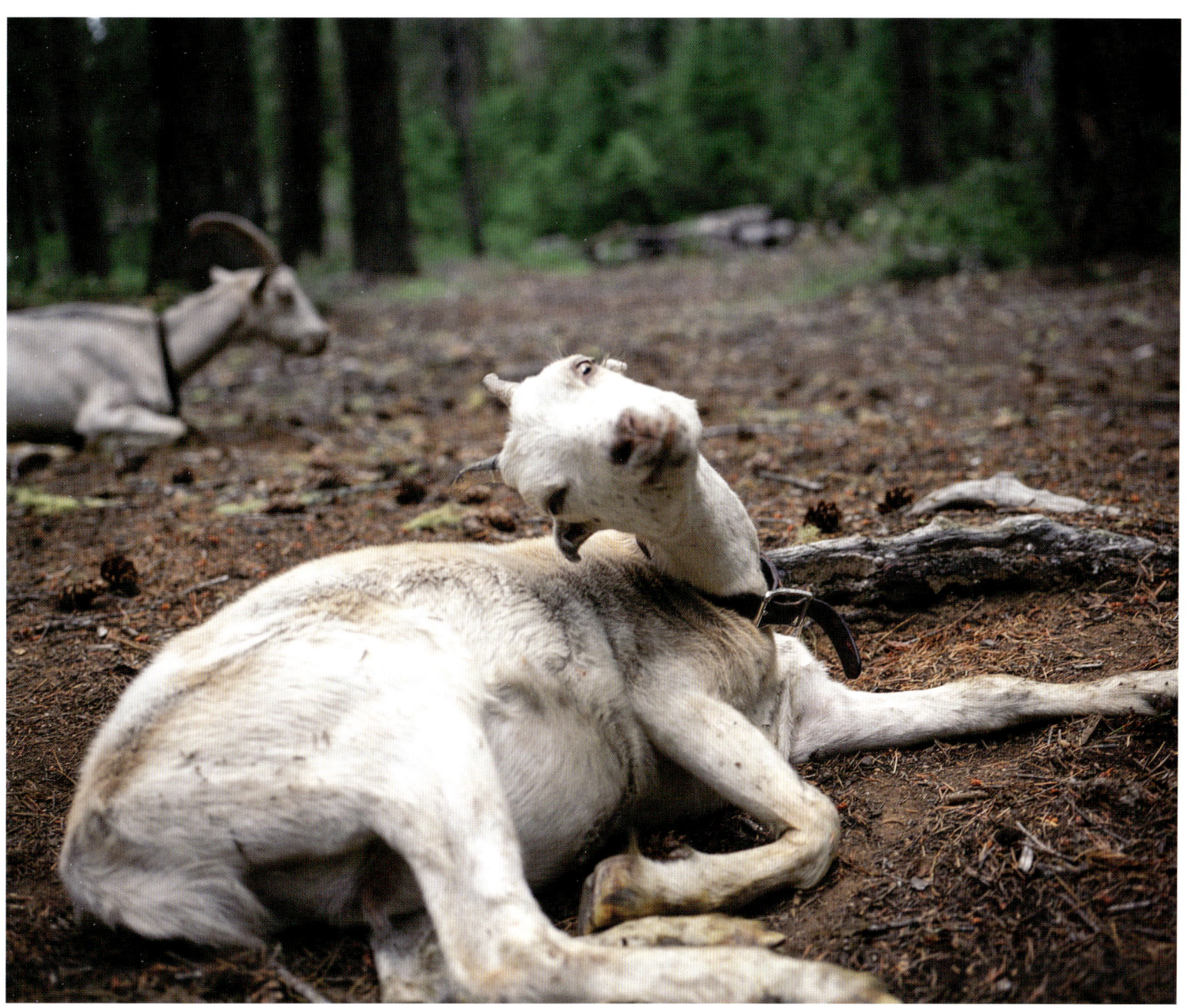

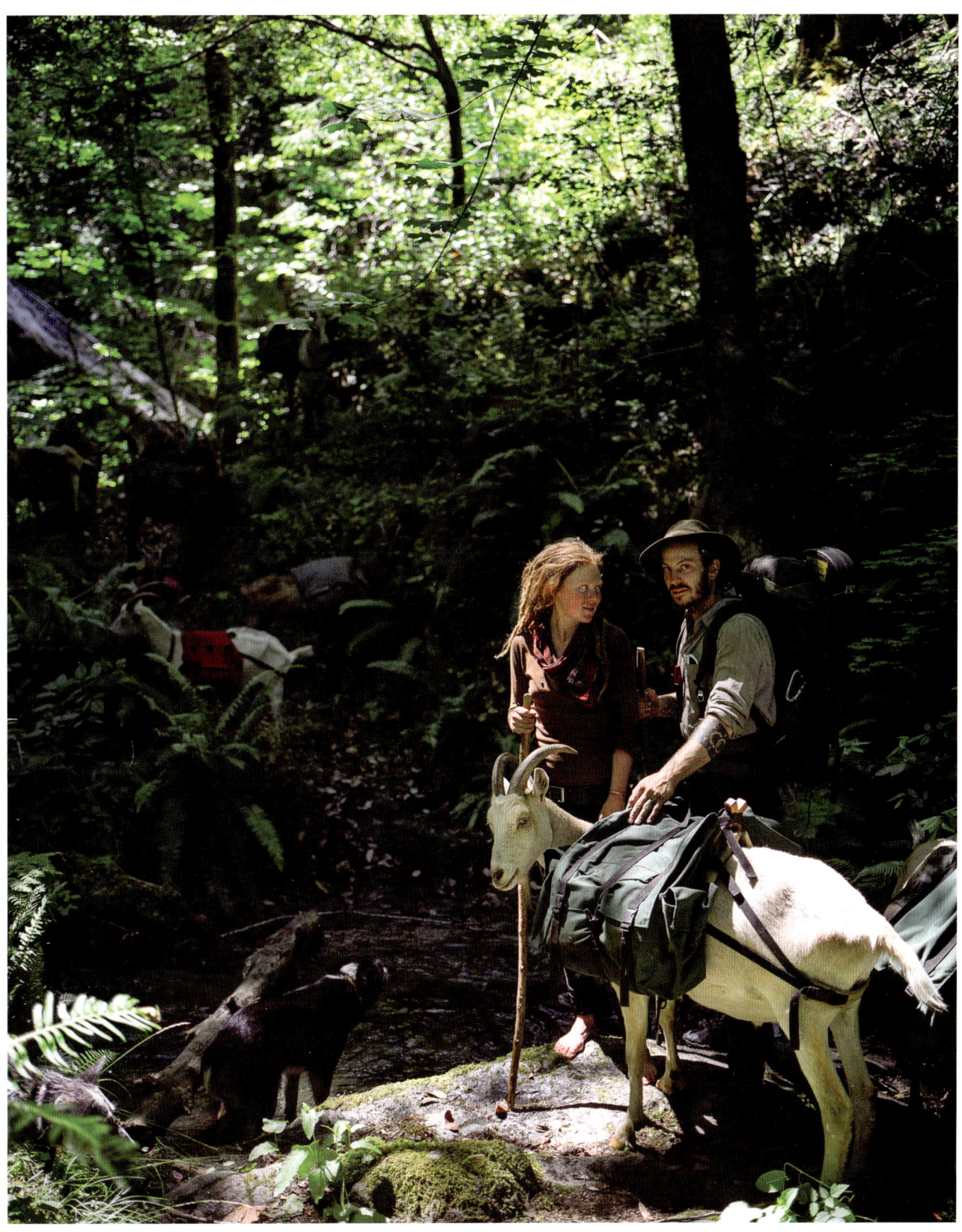

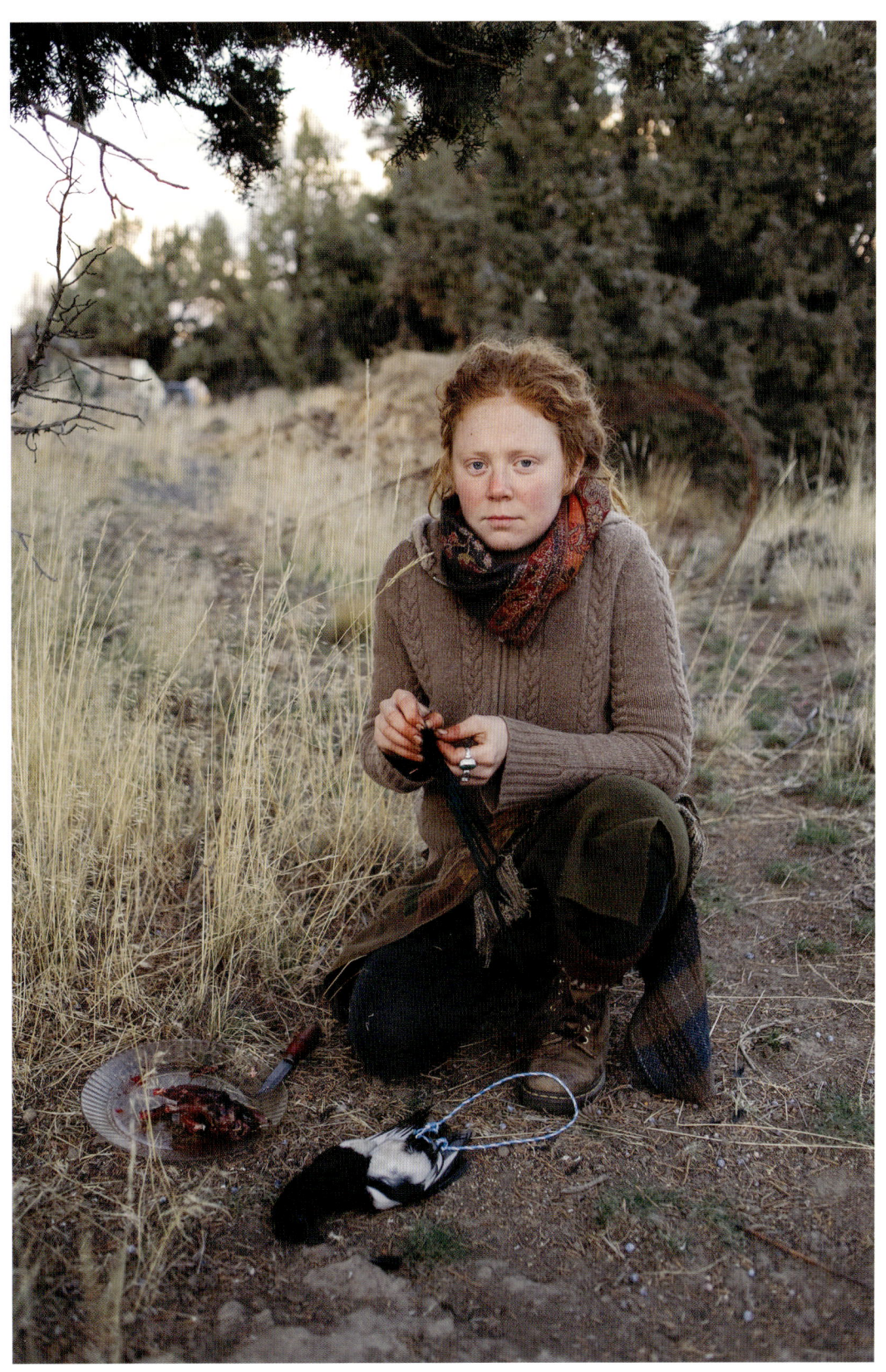

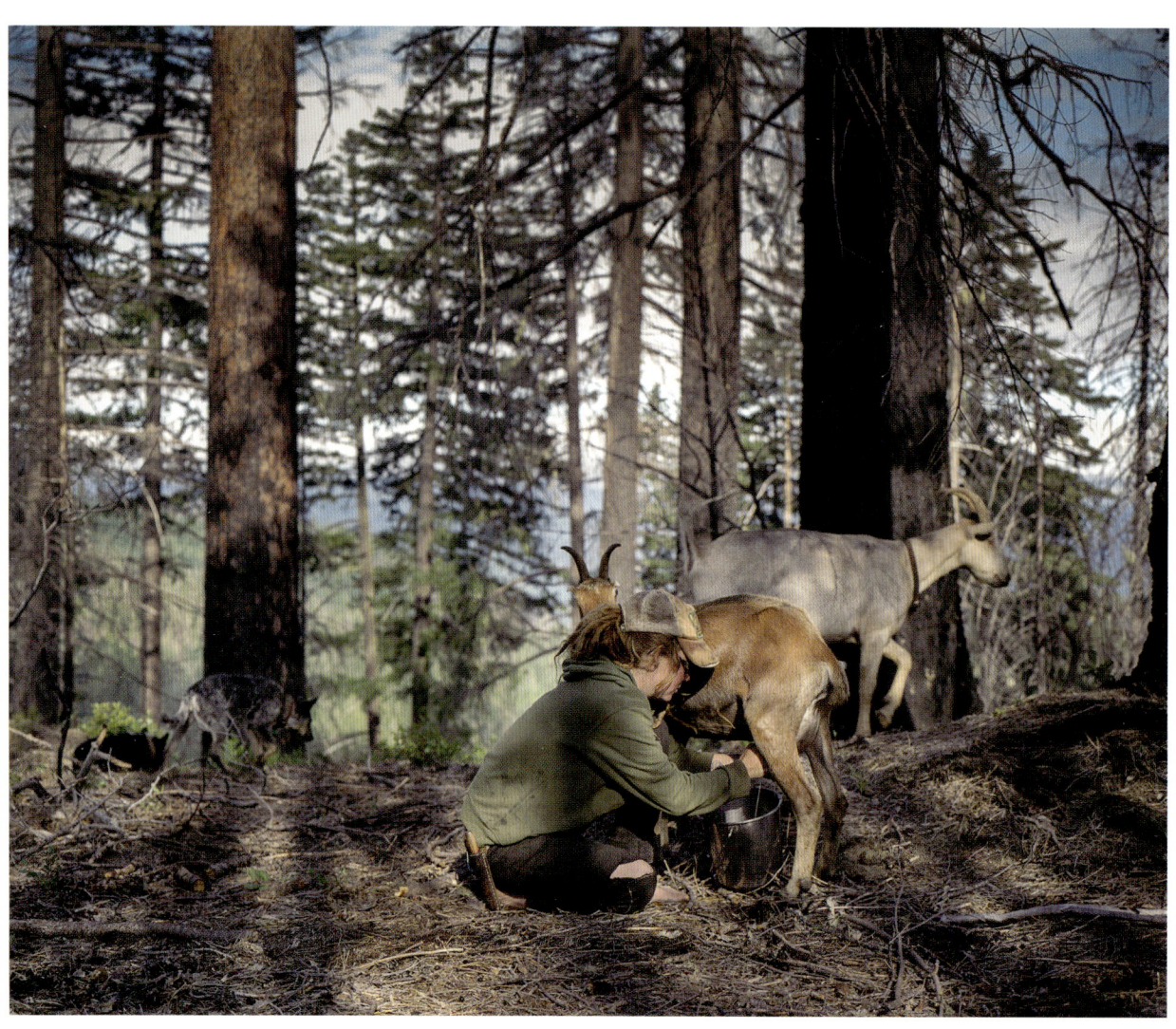

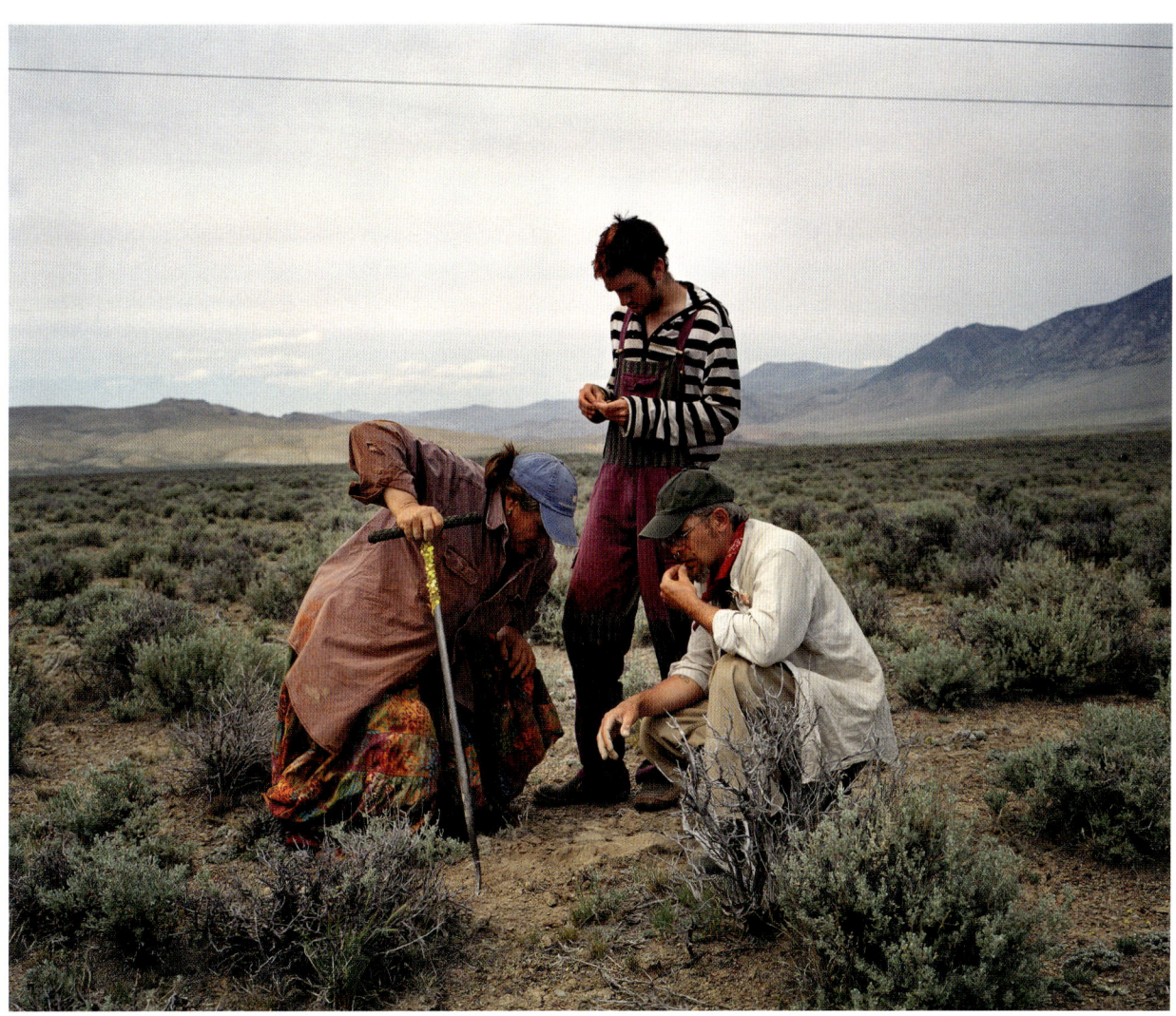

We are standing in the camas prairie at dusk with Finisia; she teaches the story of this land. Lying beneath our feet is the work of countless Bannock and Shoshone grandmothers who planted and harvested camas and breadroot for thousands of years. The harvest–a positive interaction with the plants, giving the seeds back into the earth–year after year has turned this vast prairie into a rich garden of food.

Each year they would come at midsummer, the flowers all gone to seed, and the earth dry and hard. Simply digging for food earlier in the year would have been much easier. The earth still soft and damp, the roots would come up with ease, but there would be no seeds.

We are here now to give back more than we take. We are learning the life cycle and when to harvest the roots: after the seeds are dry and ready to be planted. We struggle with the dry earth; we dig a narrow hole; we pull up a chunk of earth, the clod studded with breadroot and camas. With an easy gesture we pull the dry seeds from the plant top and drop them back into the hole. We collect the roots and tamp the soil back down. A simple action, an ancient prayer: "May there be food for the generations to come." Those roots are our supper and those roots are the legacy of all the grand-mothers who planted before.

In the distance a freeway rumbles, trucks filled with food and things, and people in cars moving on their way. We stand alone on the prairie; it is dark night now. The sound of the ancient quiet wild and the hum of modern humanity mix. Finisia sits with the patience of an old man, waiting for heroes to follow her into the wild.

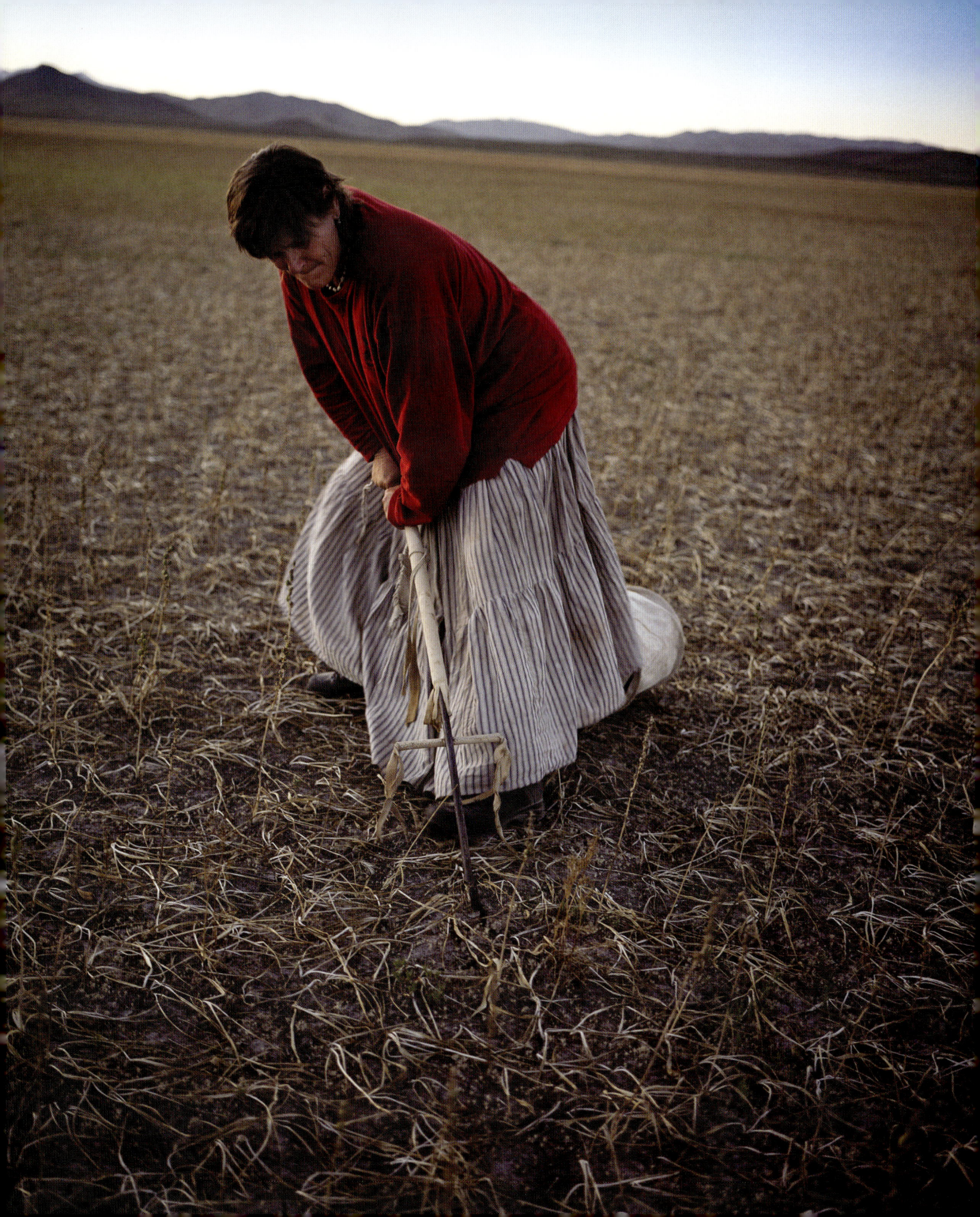

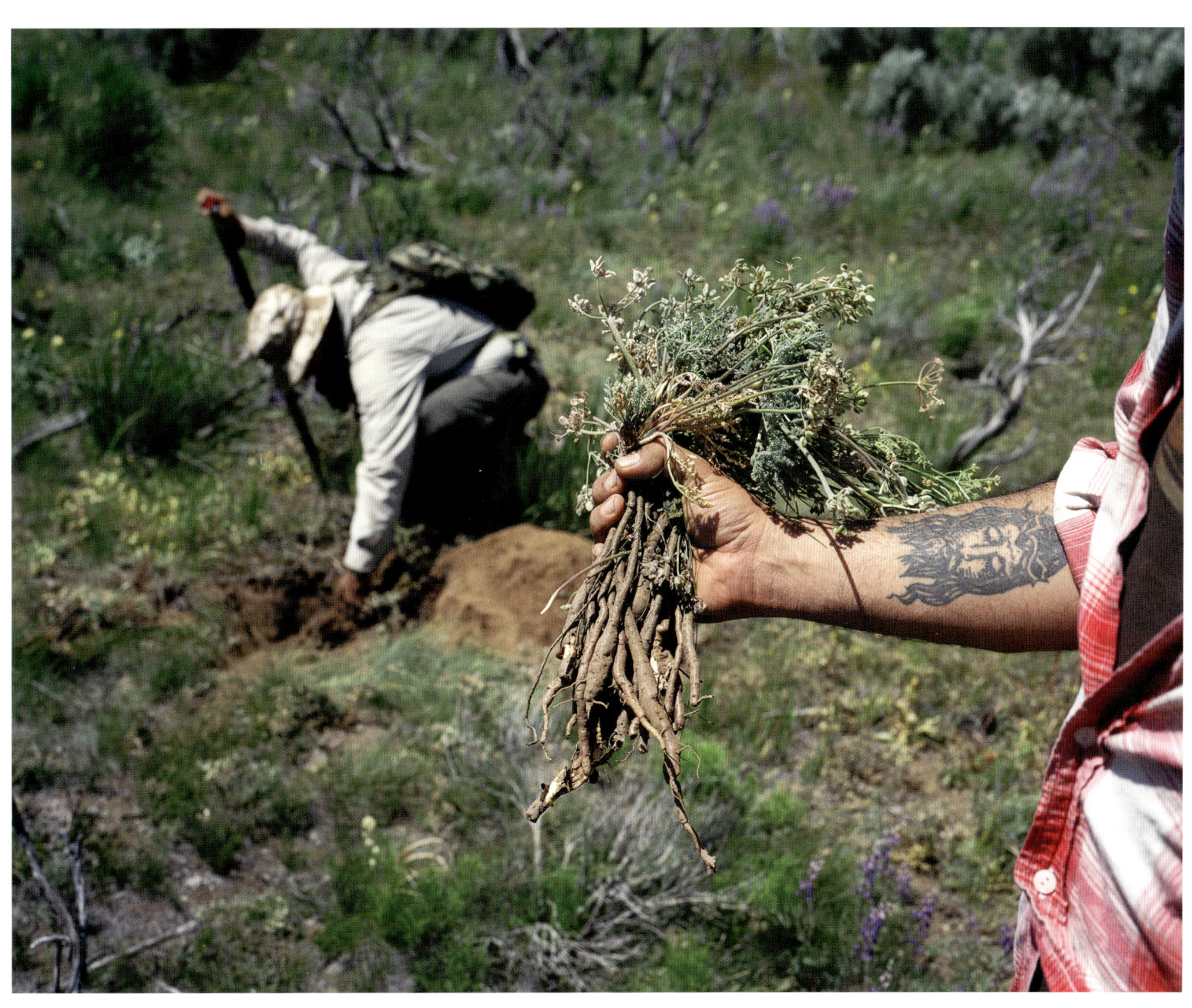

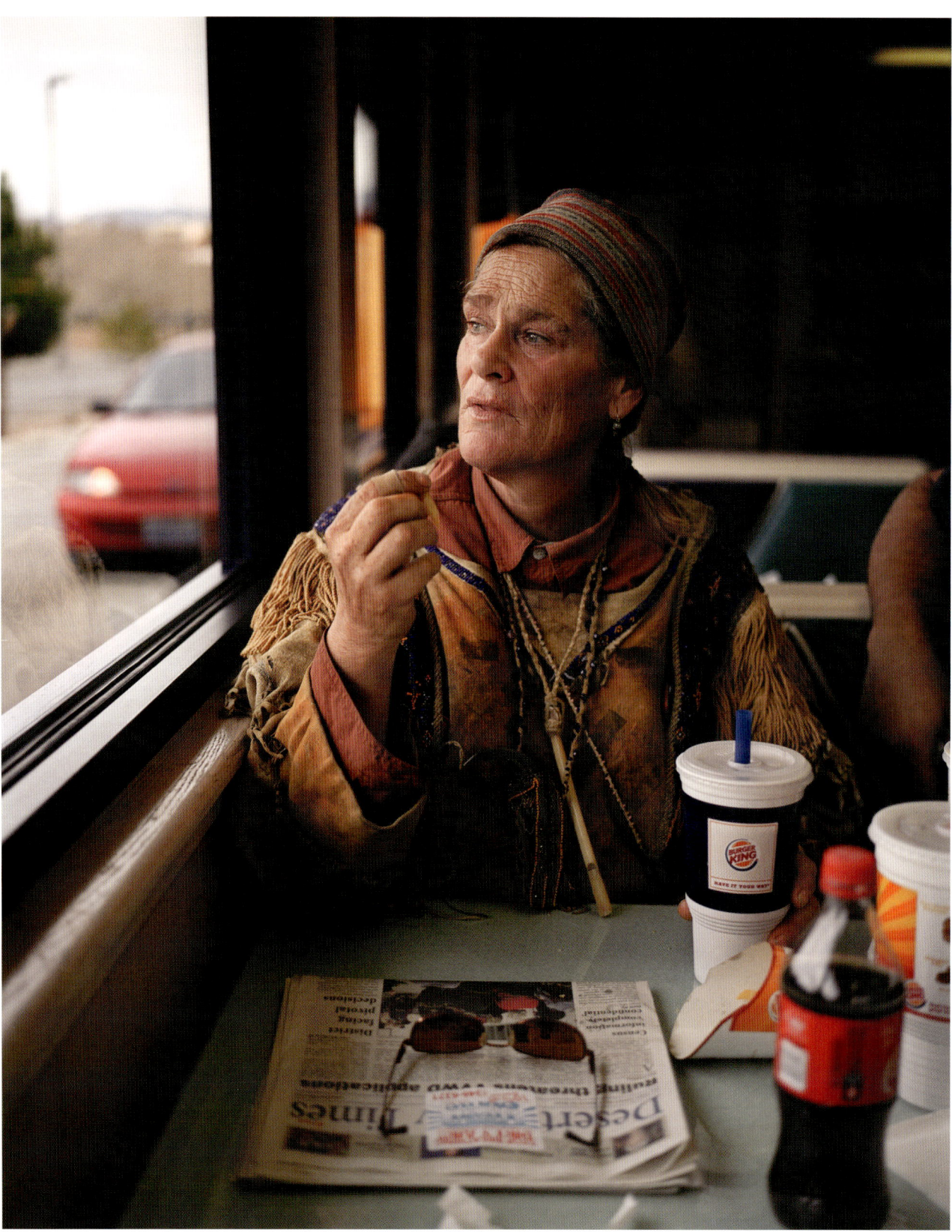

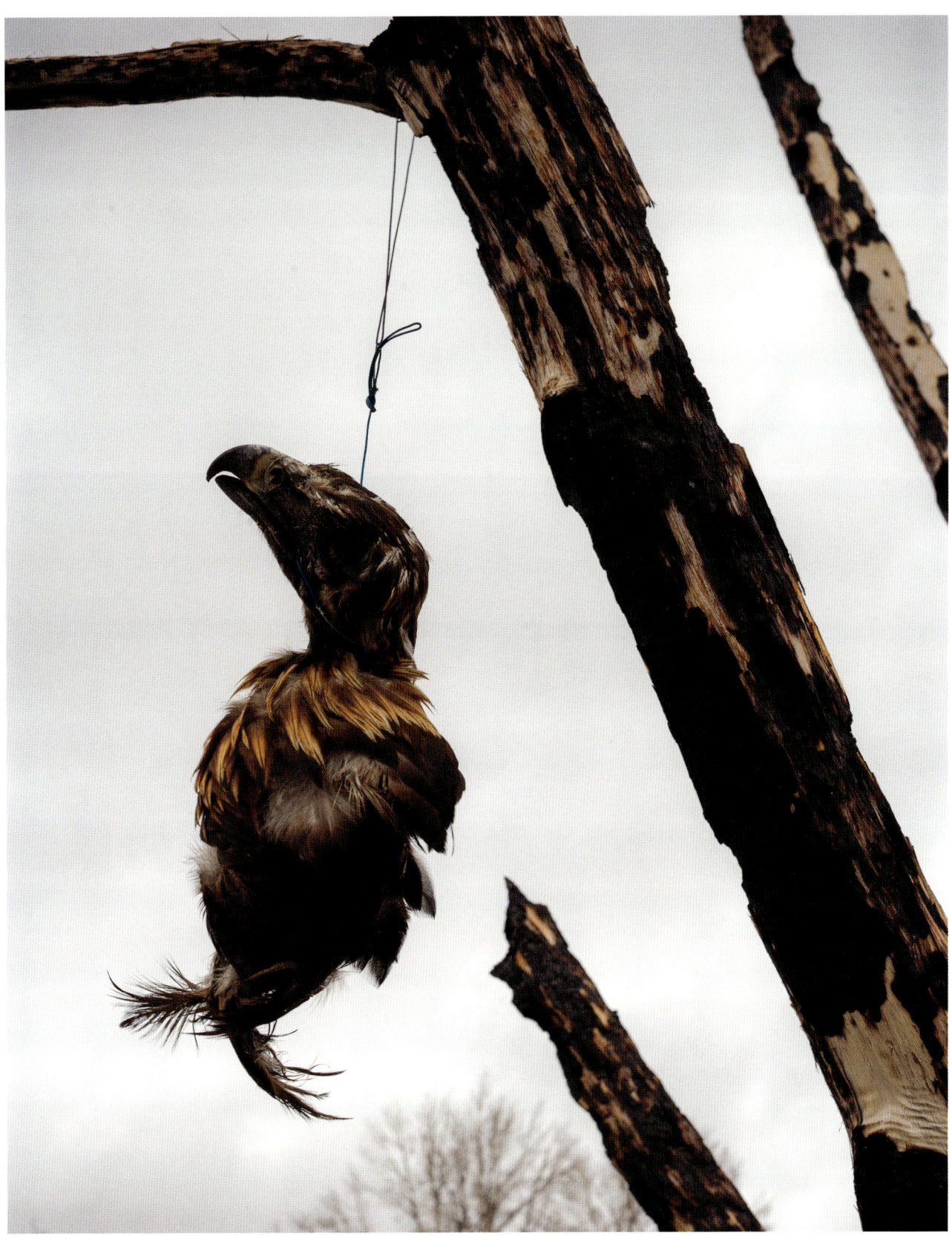

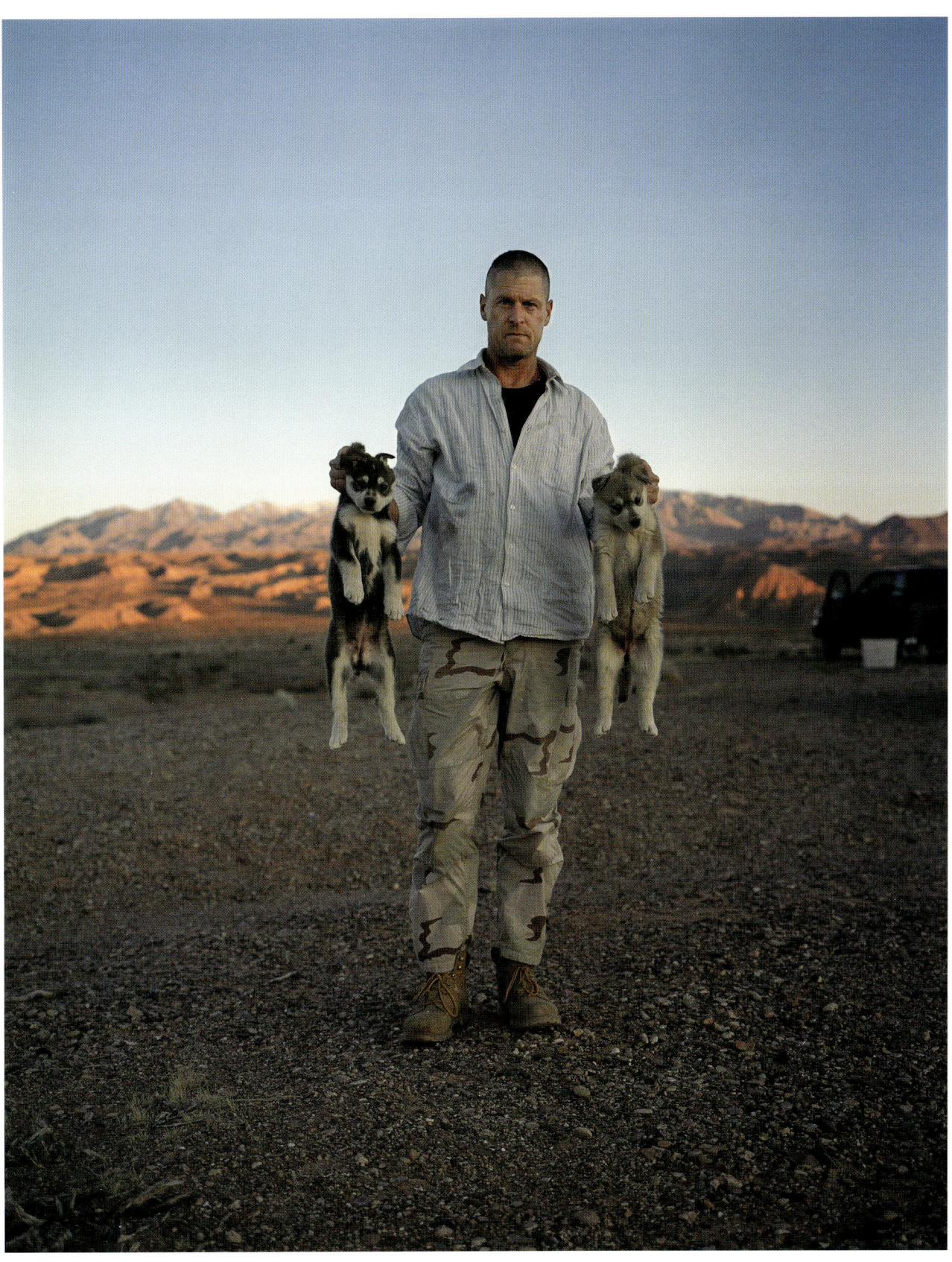

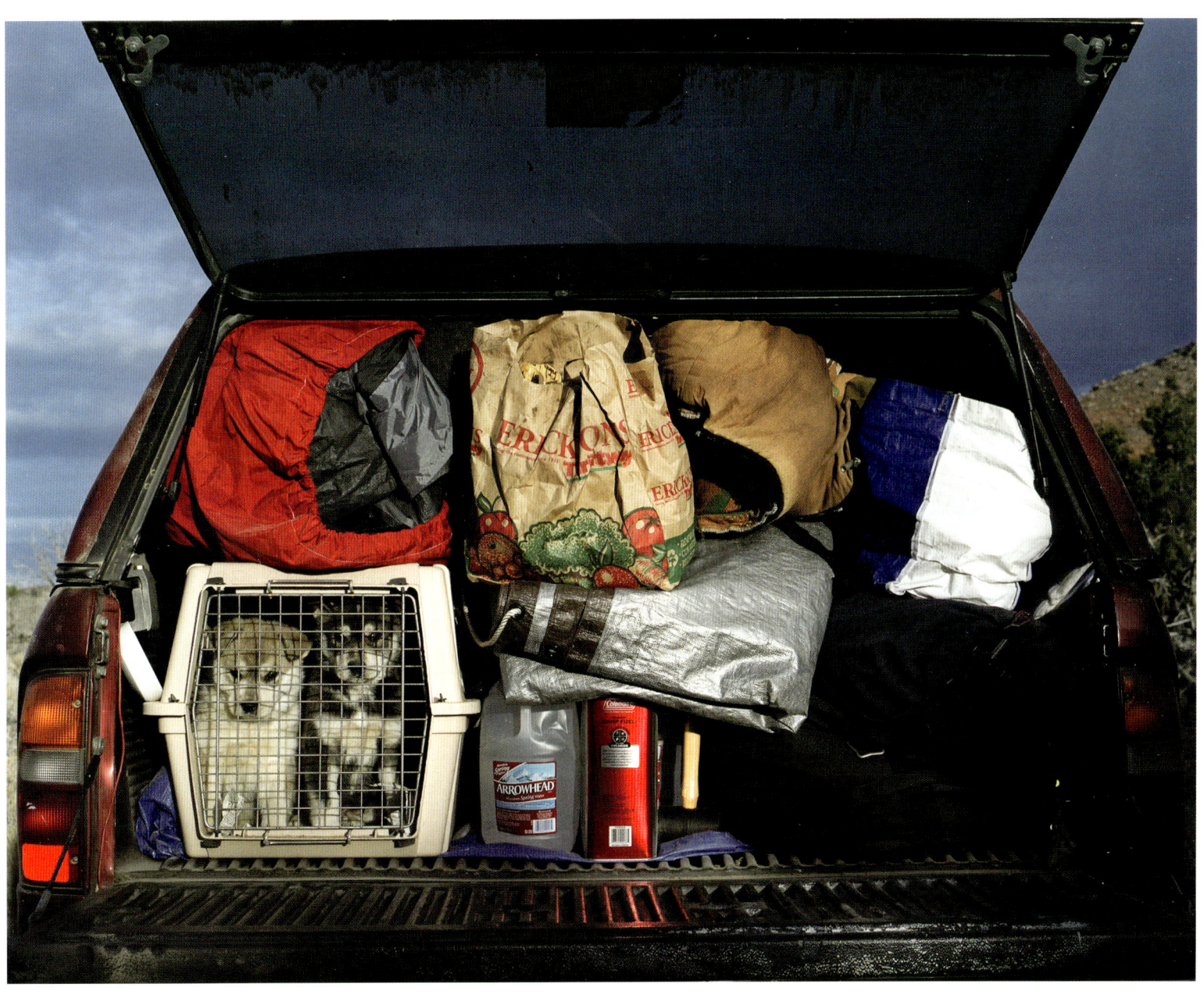

Long ago a new thing came onto the land. In the beginning it looked like a new kind of people. But as the First People watched, they became certain that it was really a monster, and they gave it the name Heart Eater Monster. Heart Eater Monster ate everything in its path. It killed all the animals it could. It ripped Mother Earth wide open and dug inside her. The First People had never seen a thing like this before. It cut through forests. It seemed to be constantly hungry and constantly growing. Wave after wave of the monster came upon the land. Heart Eater Monster got so big it took control. It told the First People where to live and how to be. Soon few animals remained. The people were scared and hungry.

The people went to the Elders and asked "What should we do?" The Elders held a great counsel; for four days they remained in the lodge.

They came out with a message from Spirit.

"This Heart Eater Monster is too big and powerful for us to conquer now. We must wait and watch. We must learn its magic. Watch closely what it does and how it works. You must learn how it spins so that you can one day un-spin what it has done. There will come a time when the Heart Eater Monster has eaten too much. It will become too big and too fat and it will stumble and fall. And that will be the time of the un-spinning. At that time, use what you have witnessed. Reverse the magic of the monster. Un-spin the monster.

The people have been watching and waiting. And some say the time of the un-spinning is now.

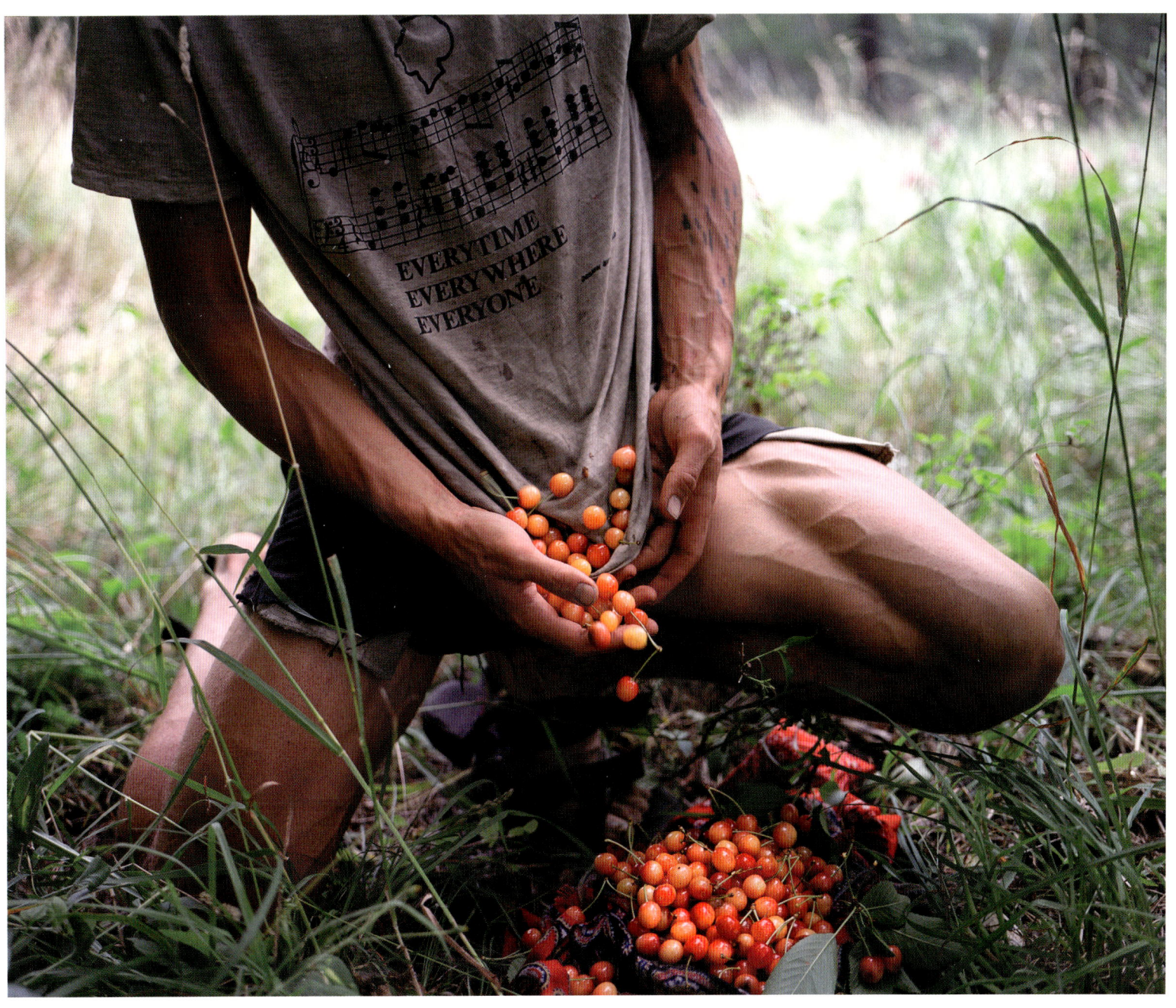

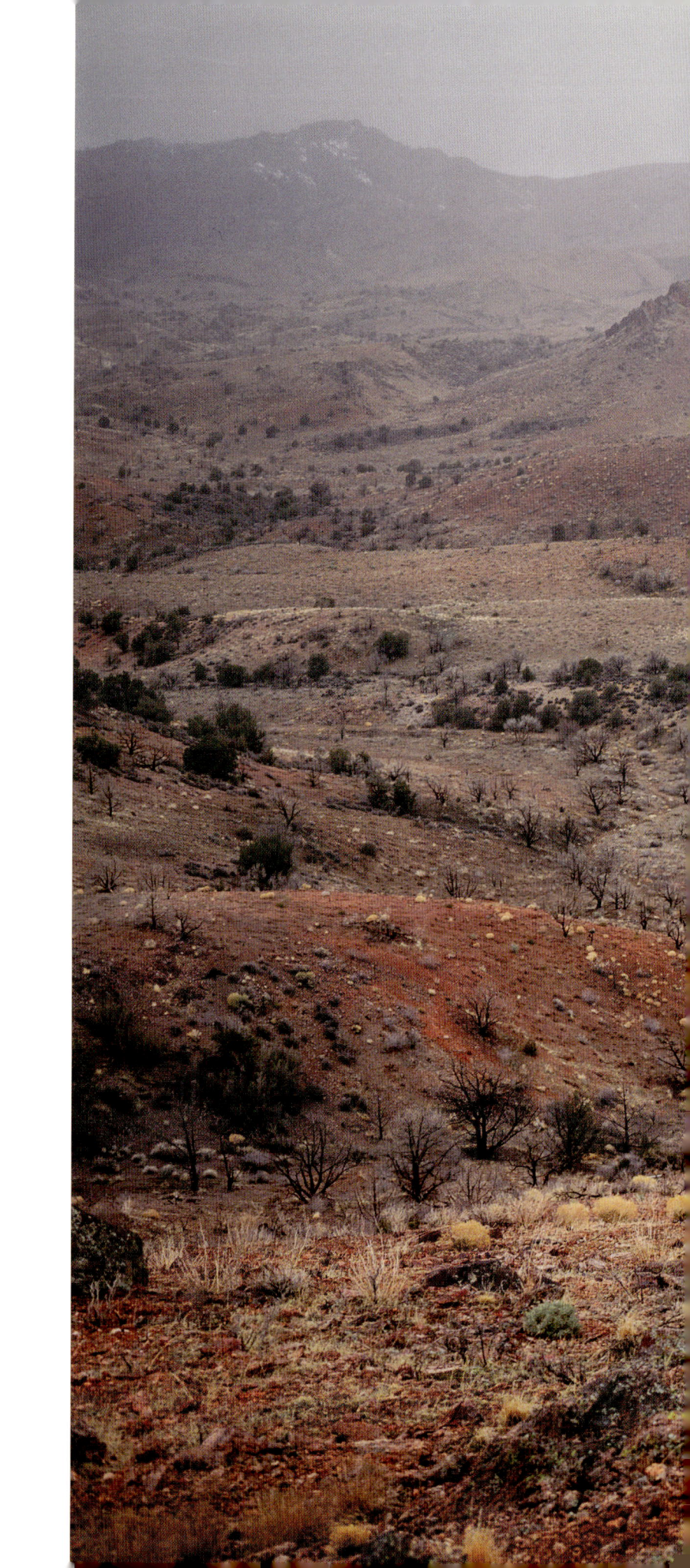

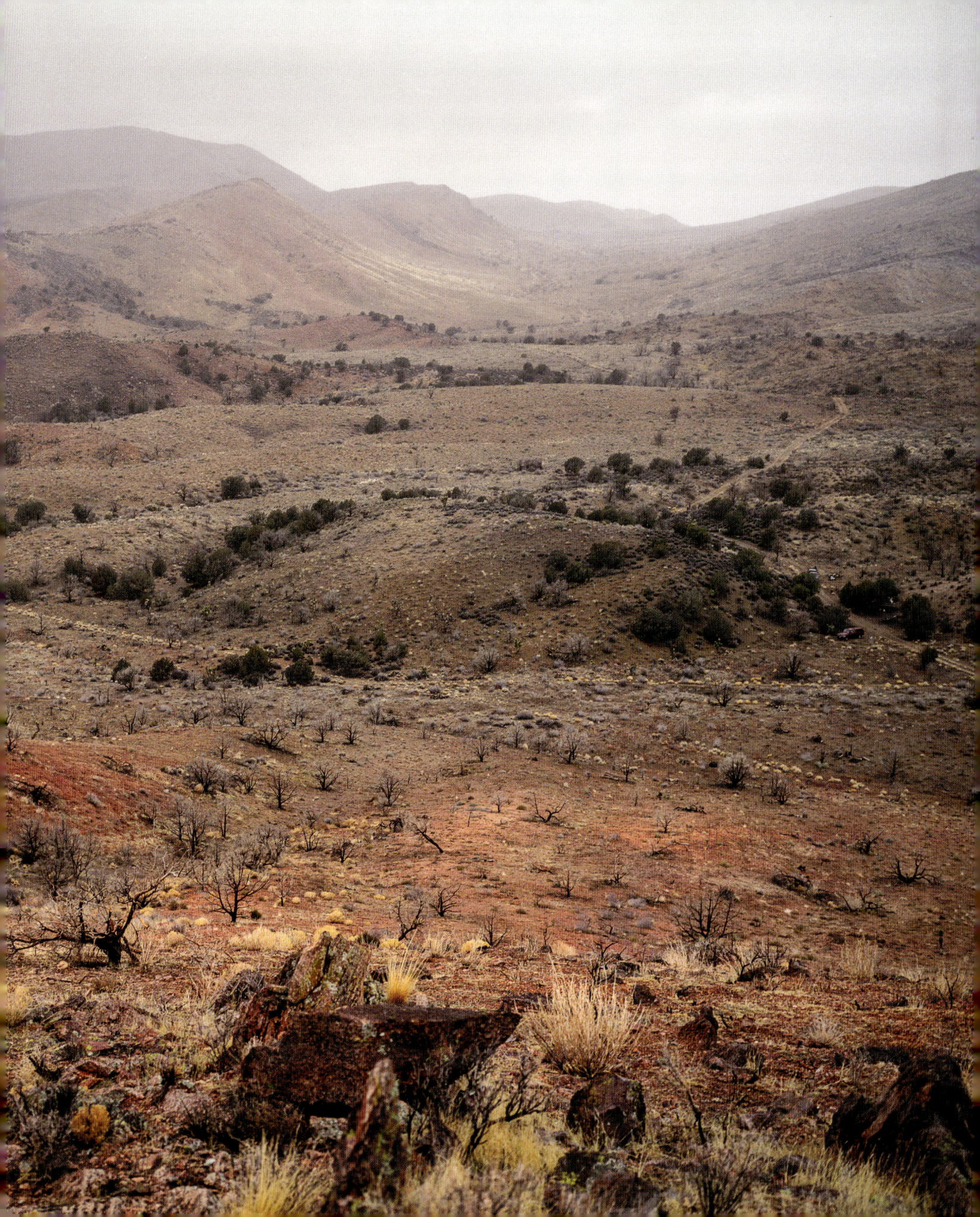

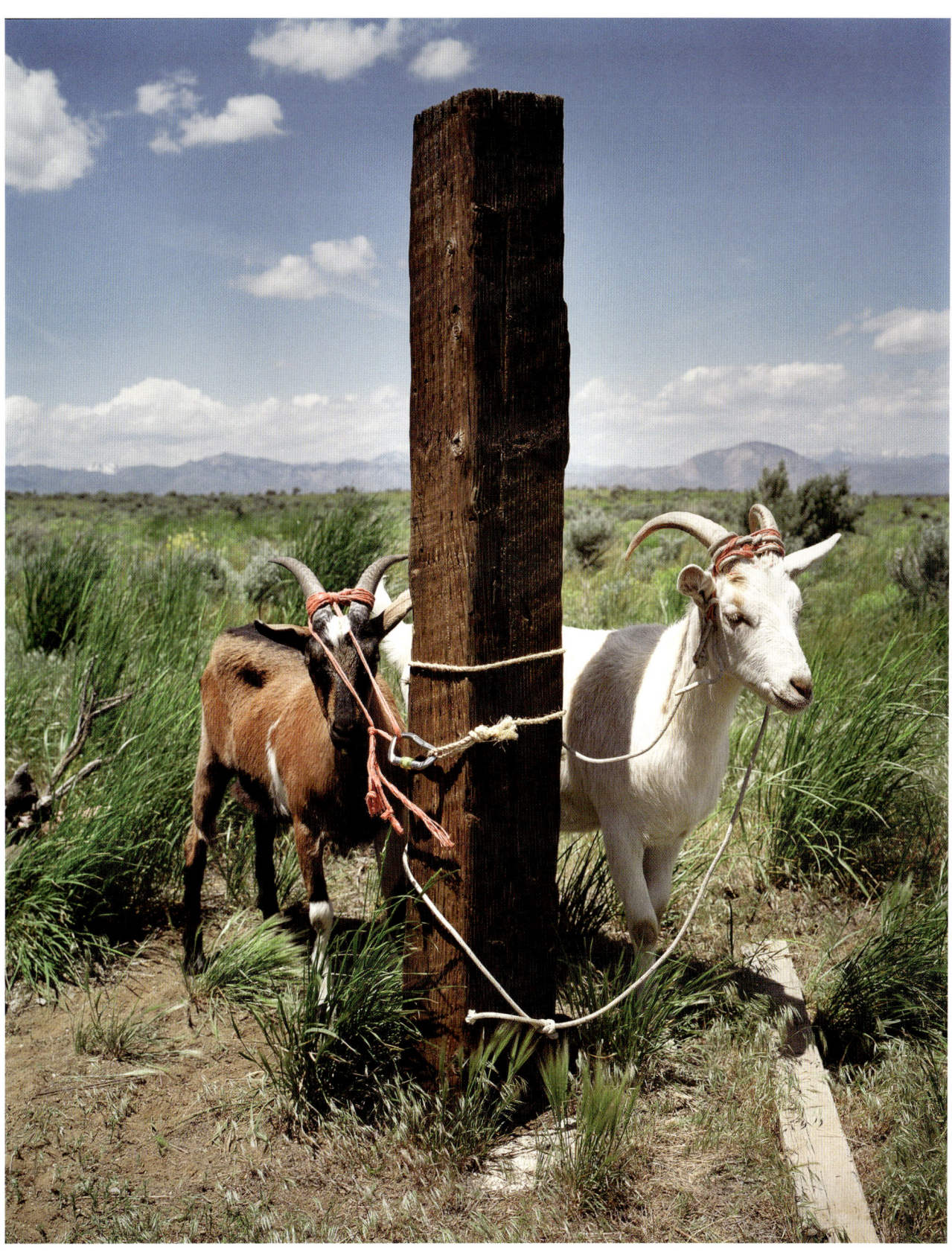

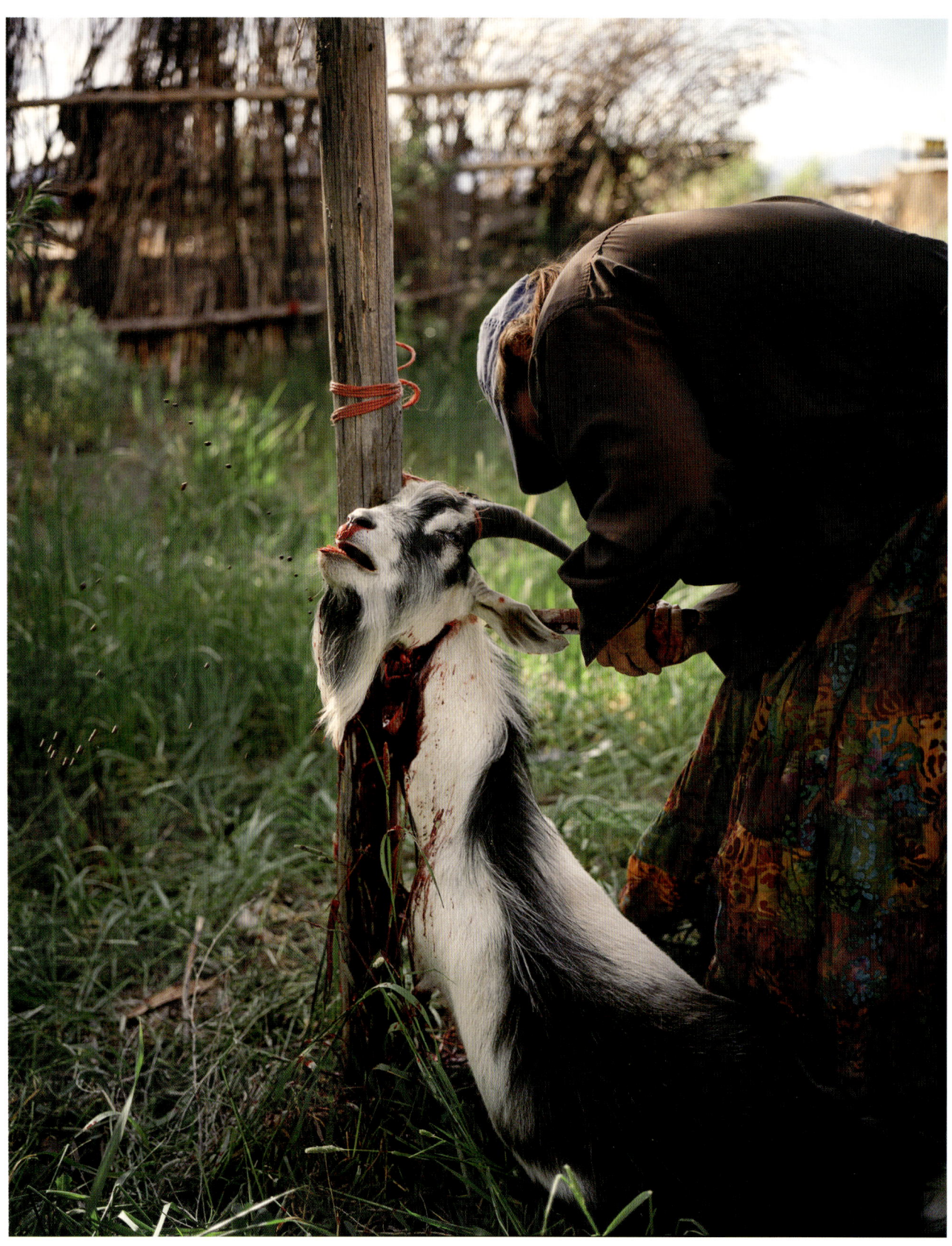

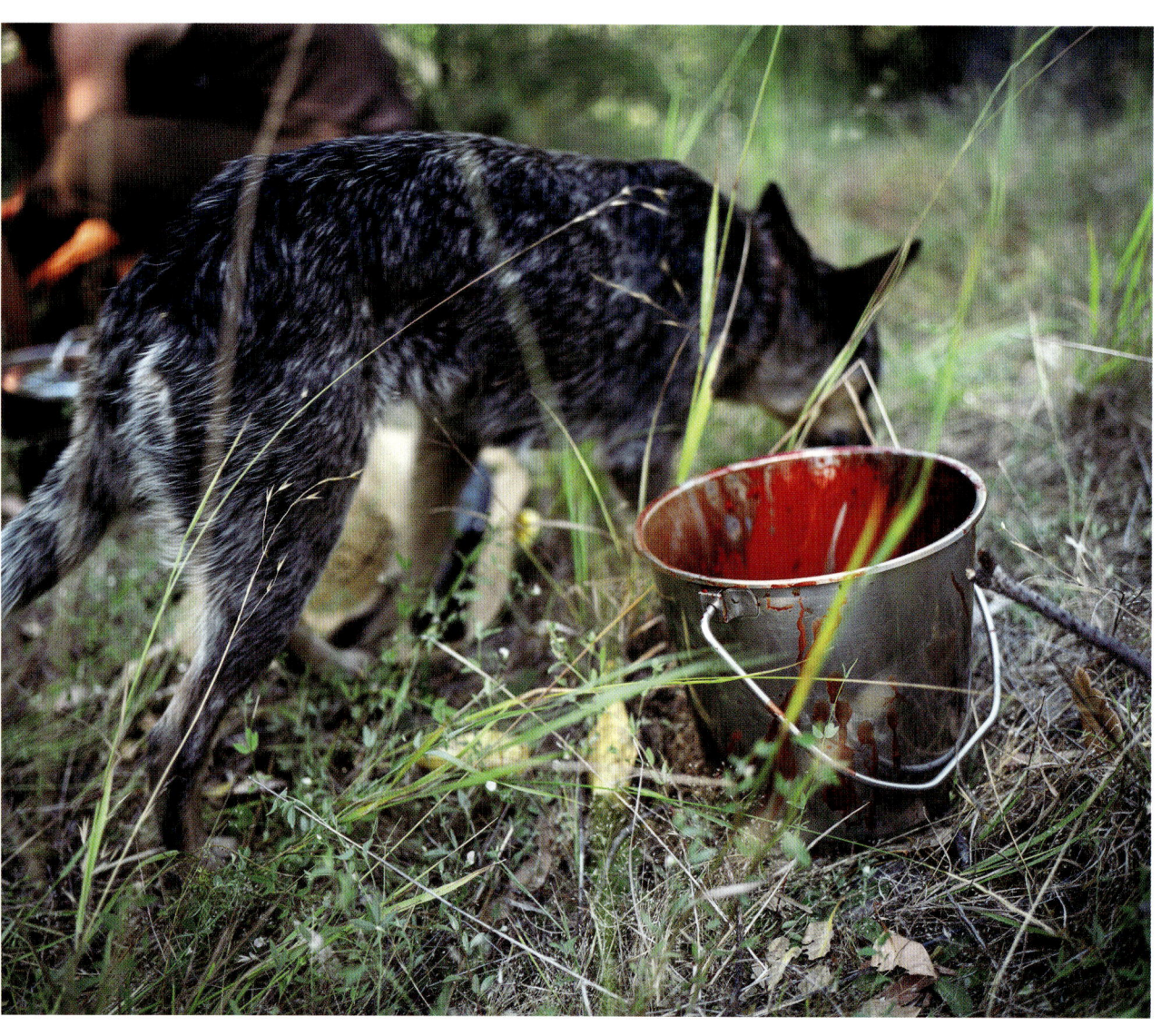

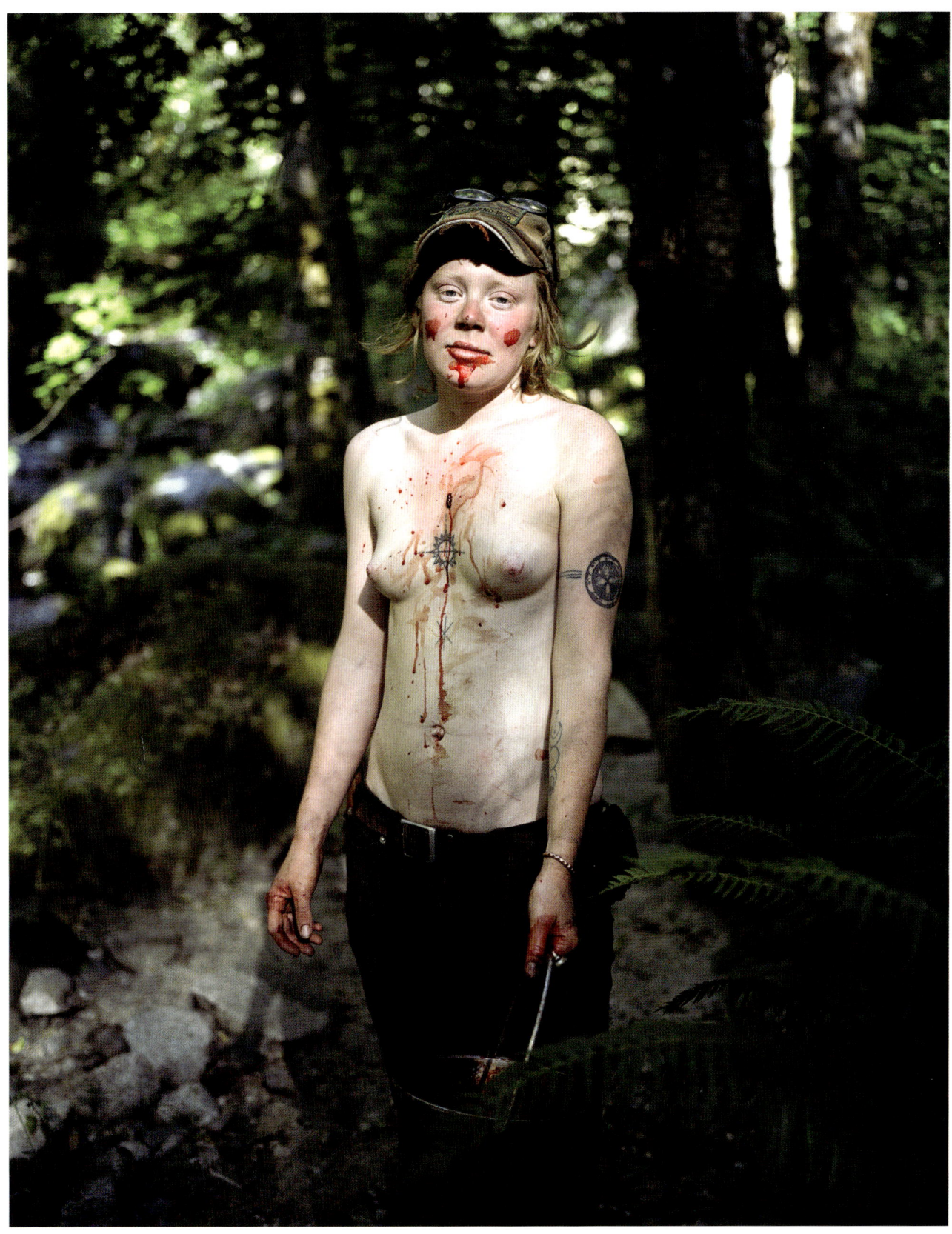

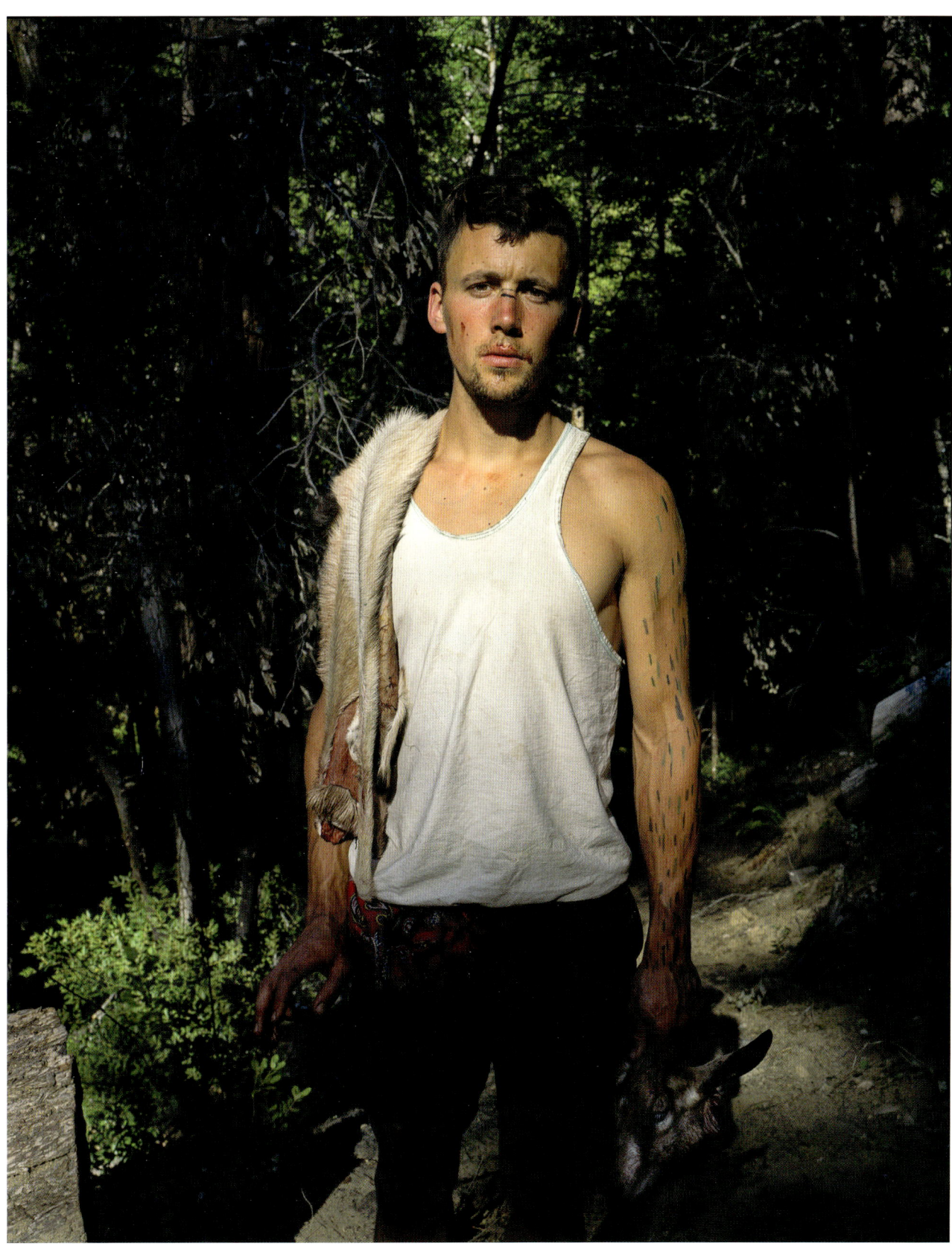

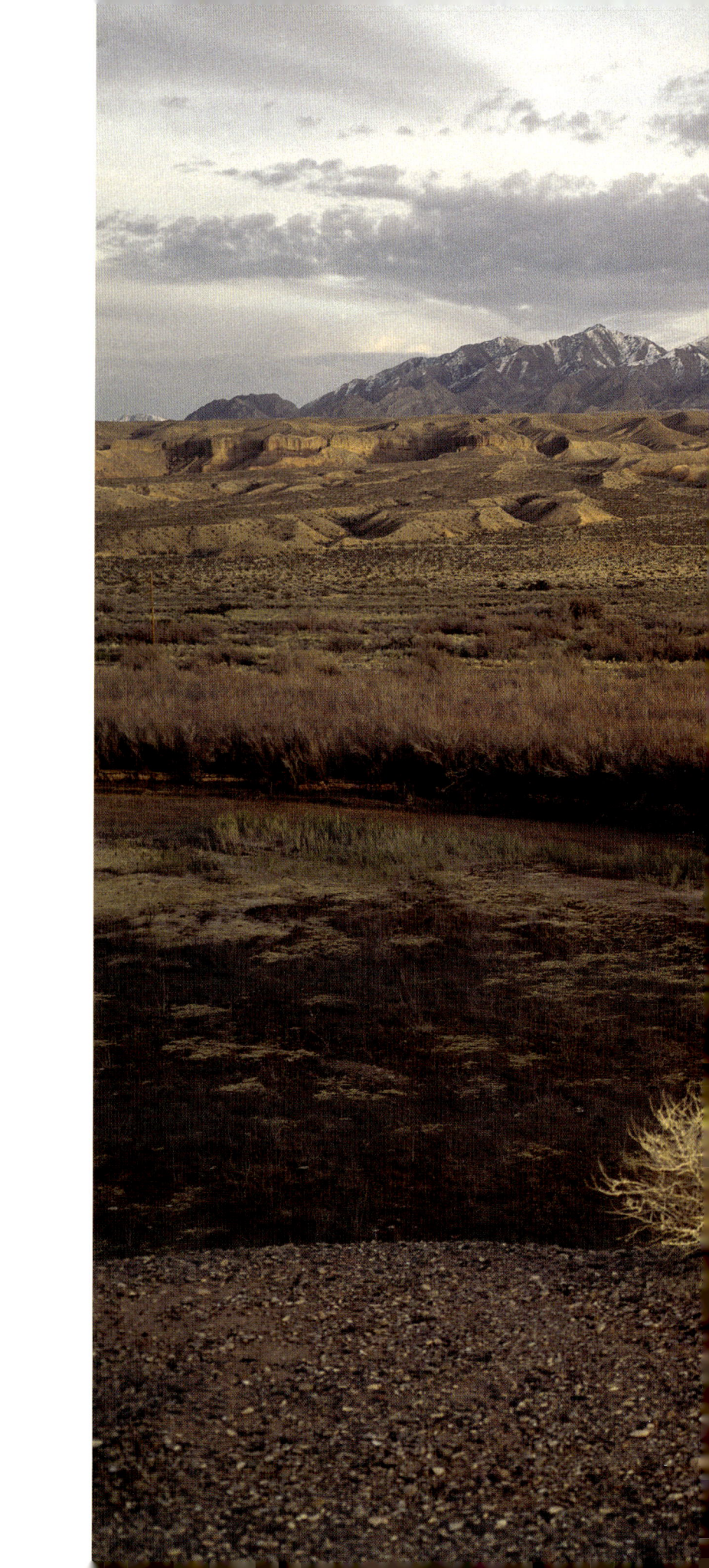

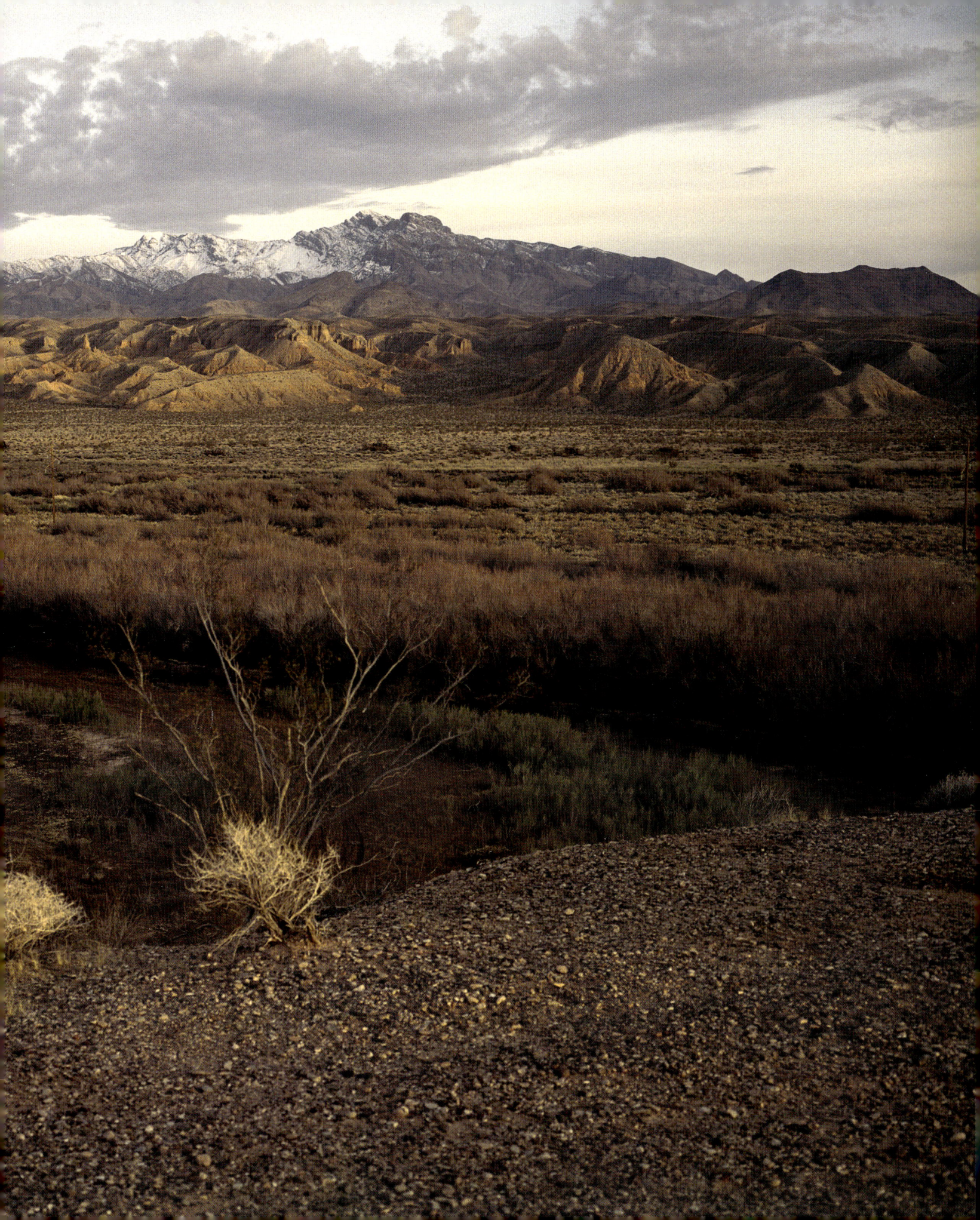

the Garden will go untended for seven generations it will be close to death
a new tribe will arise
a Rainbow tribe
the in-betweens
the dispossessed
and the heroic youth
will be the first to walk this path
this tribe and others will begin the Un-Spinning
it will take seven generations for the Return to be made complete
it will be a struggle for those who cling to what once was
strength will find those who embrace what will be
each generation will leave a layer behind
each generation will be given a gift
and so it will be until the people and the Garden are once again wild and free

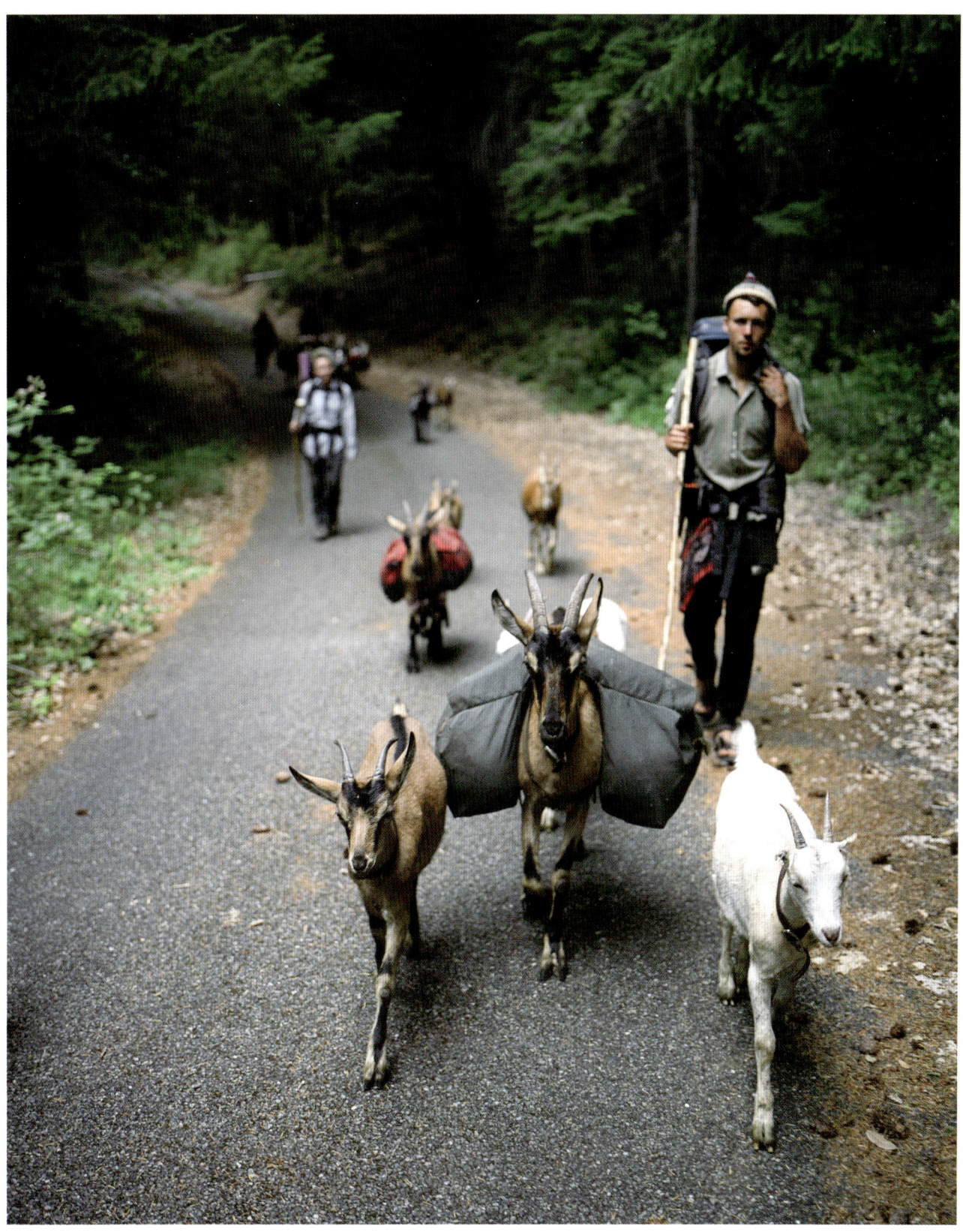

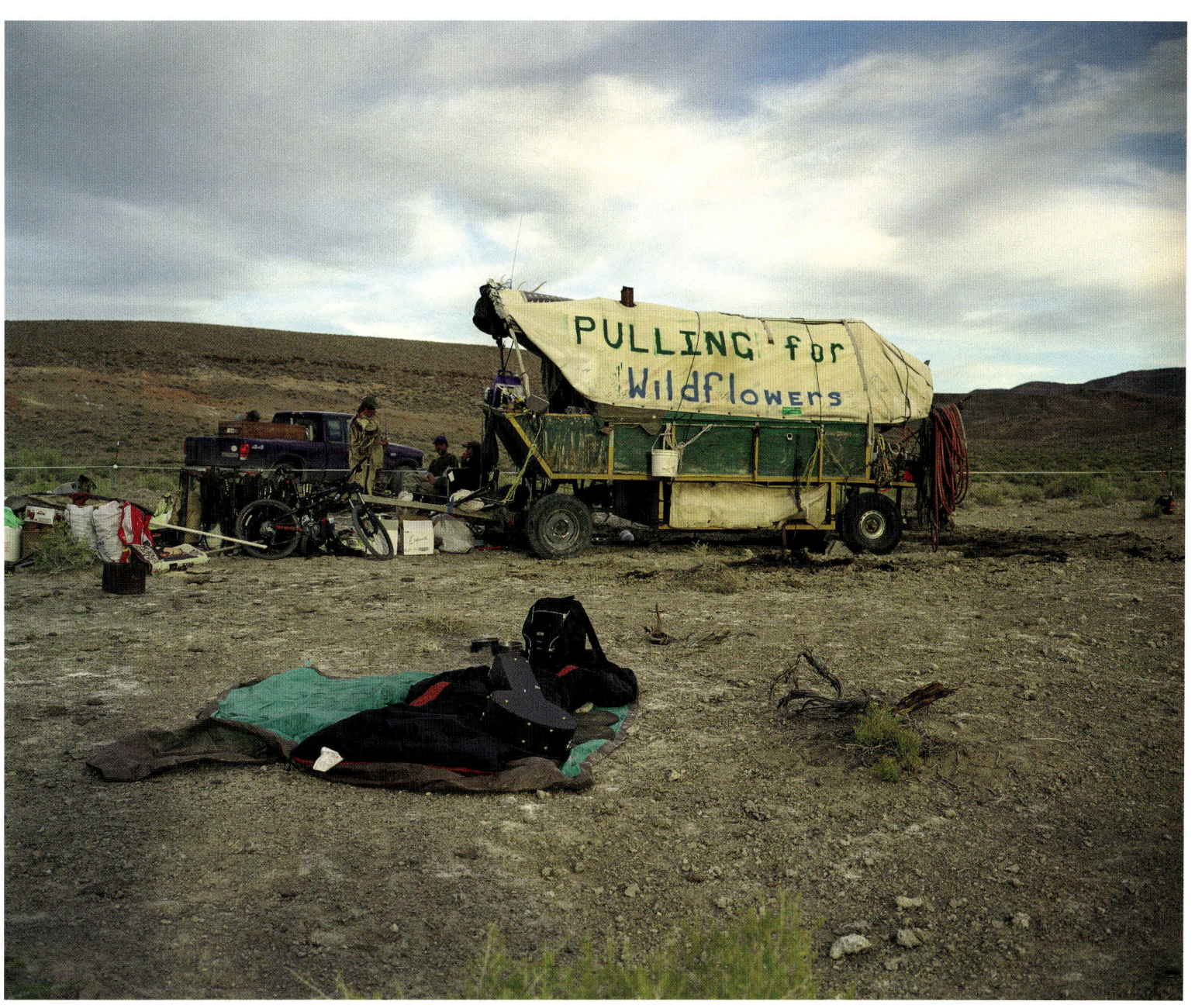

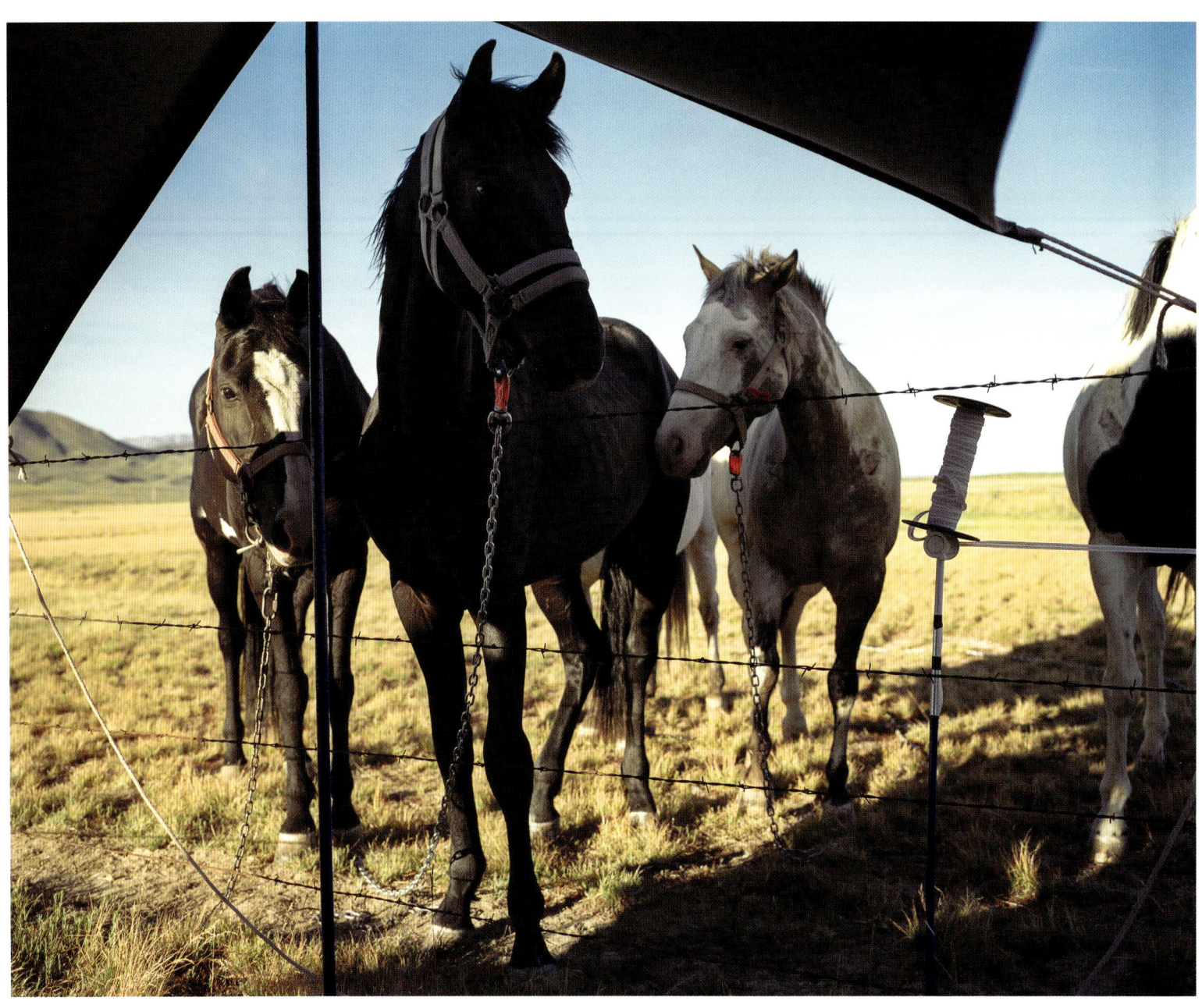

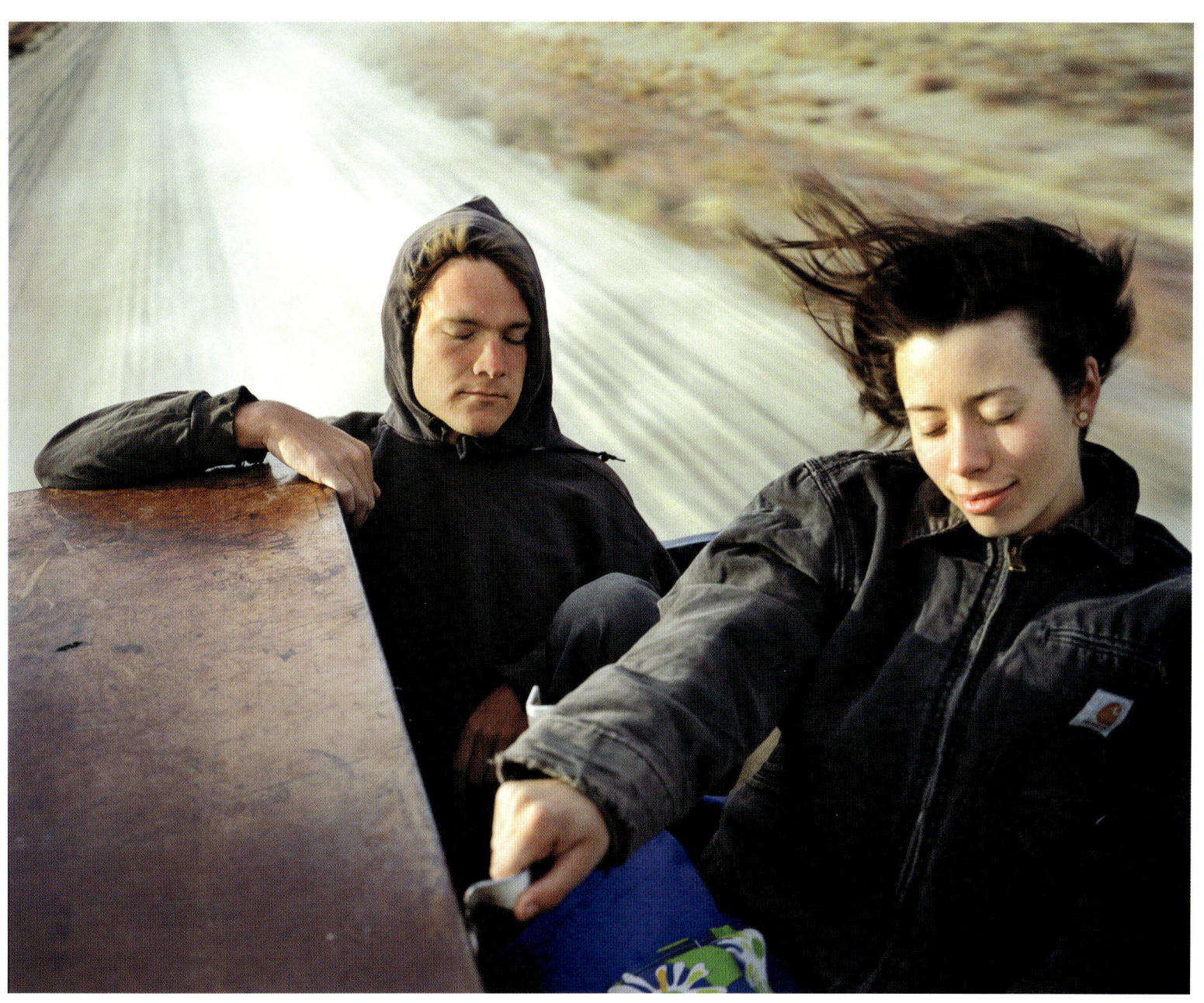

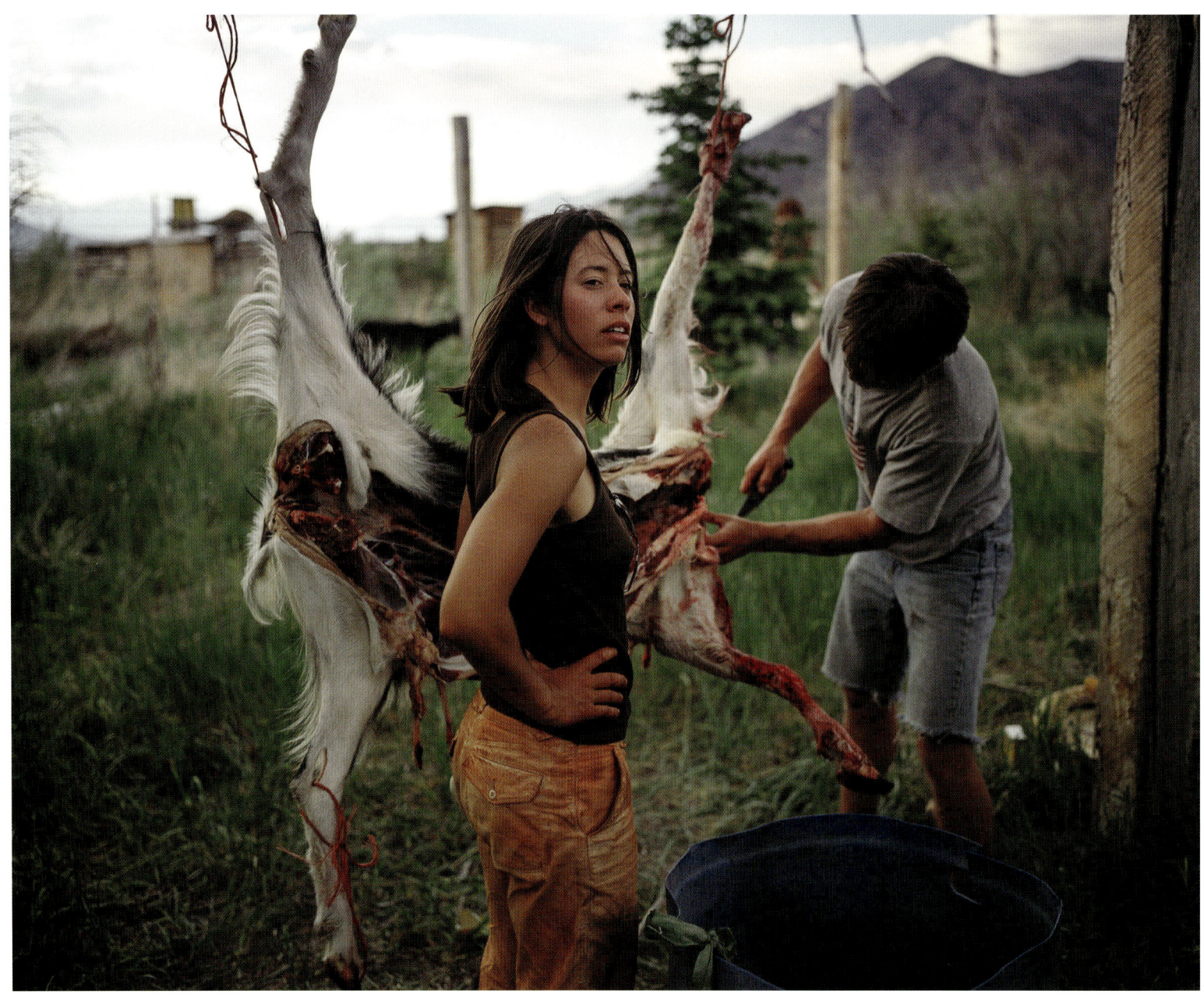

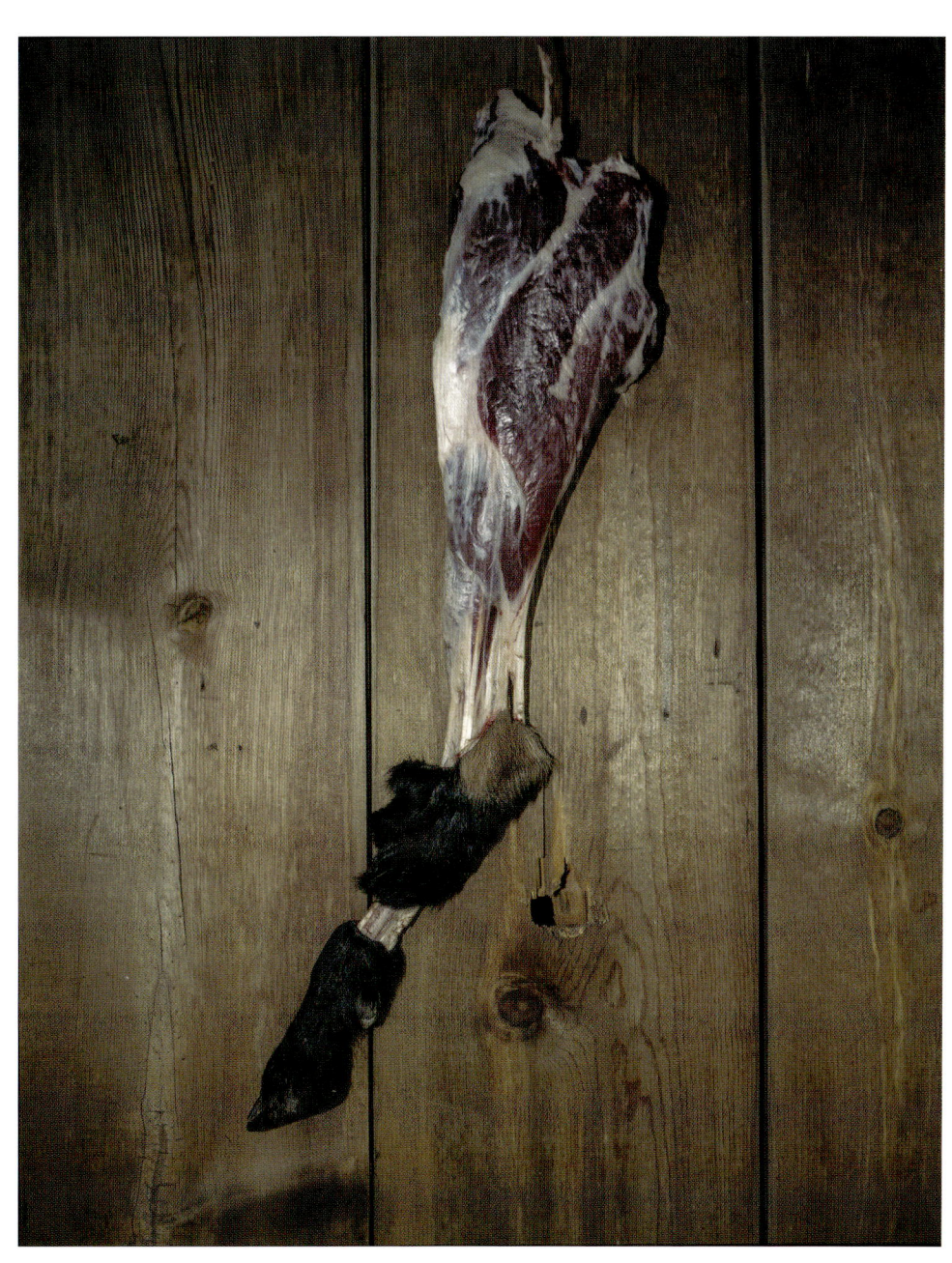

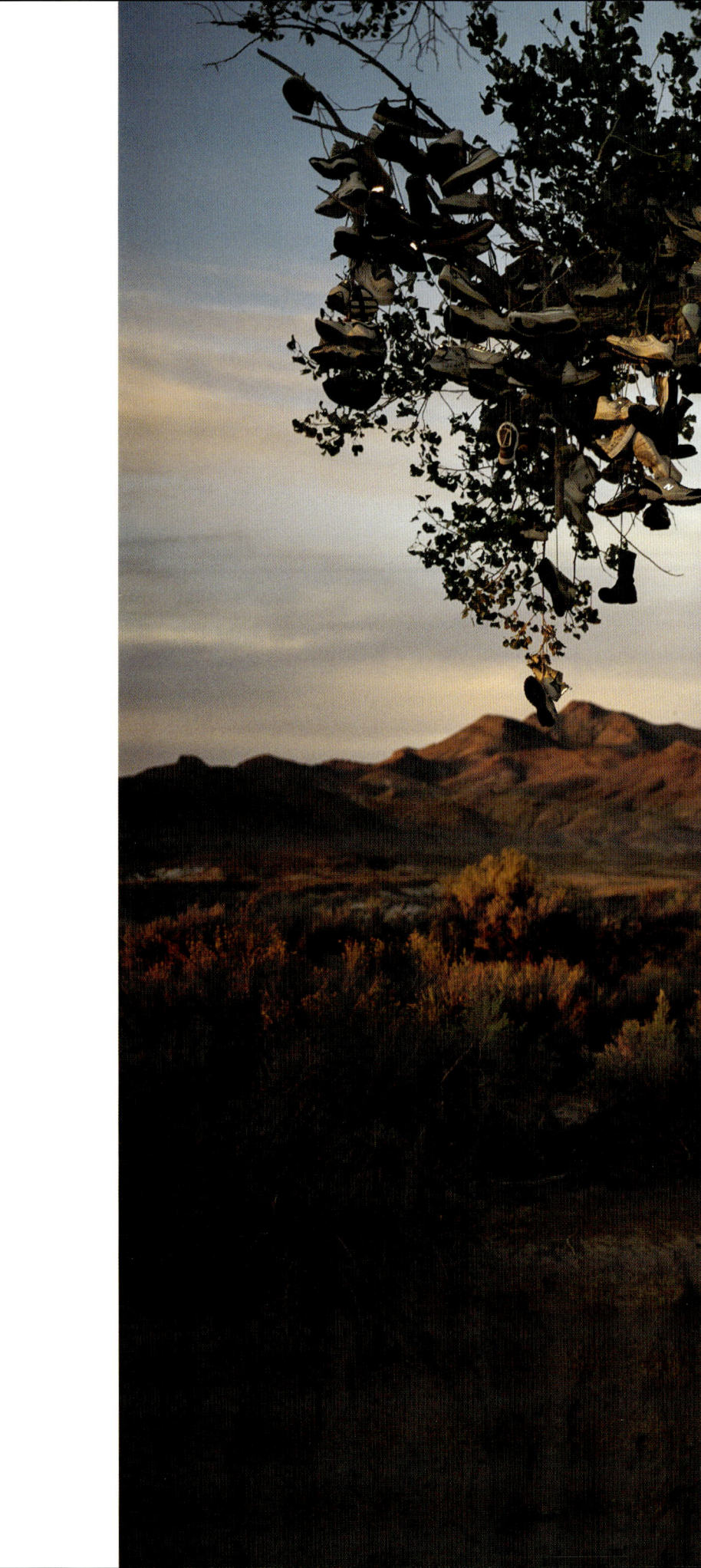

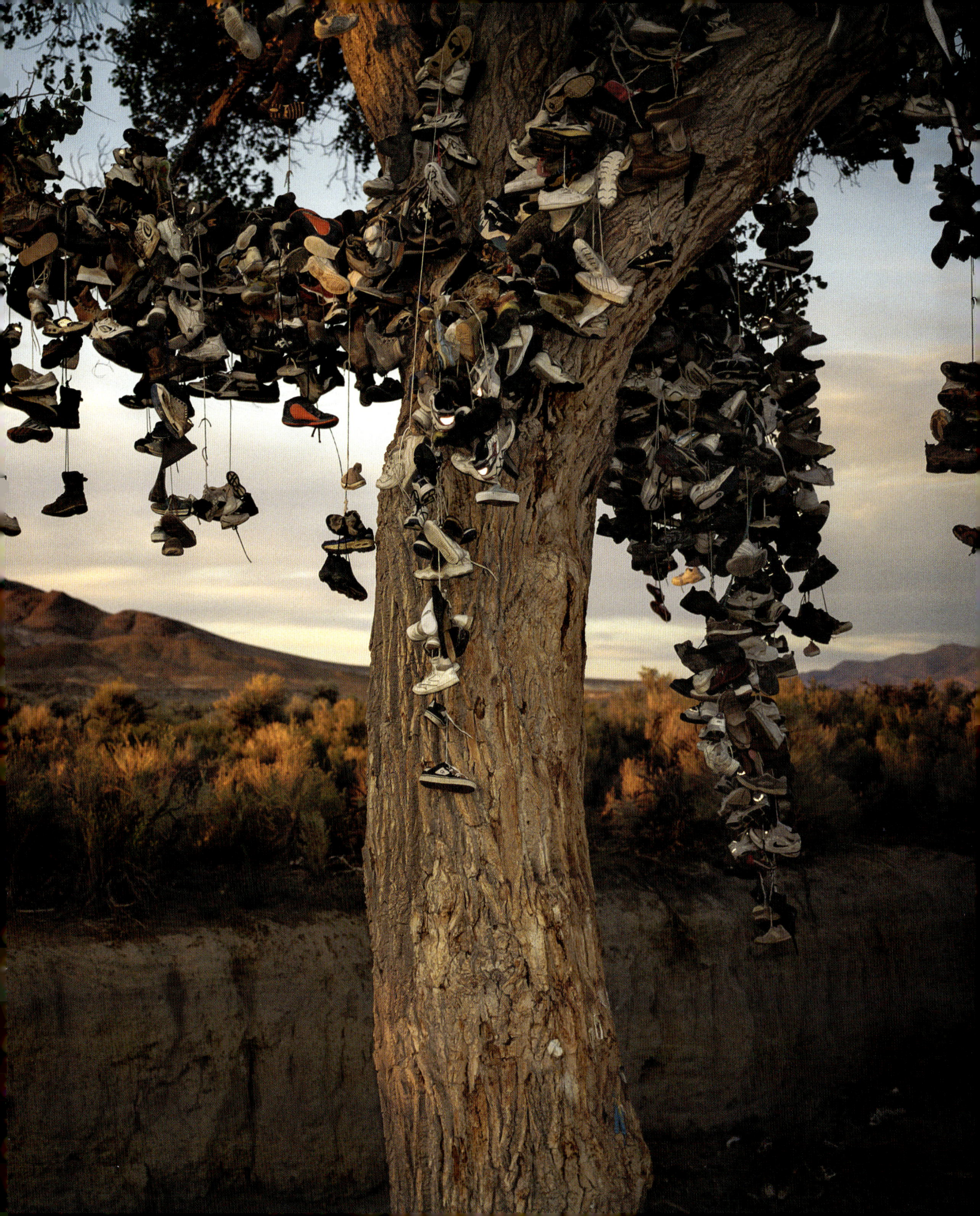

As we gain at least a small understanding of what it is to live in true harmony with the earth that sustained the human race for so long, we feel the Spirit presence in our work guiding our hands. Treating all life as equal and finding ways of creating and preserving space for nature's true diversity is a radical act that chips away at the concrete and asphalt of the industrial monoculture that has come to define much of life on the planet in the last century; and it lets us breathe an air of renewed possibilities.

—Leopard

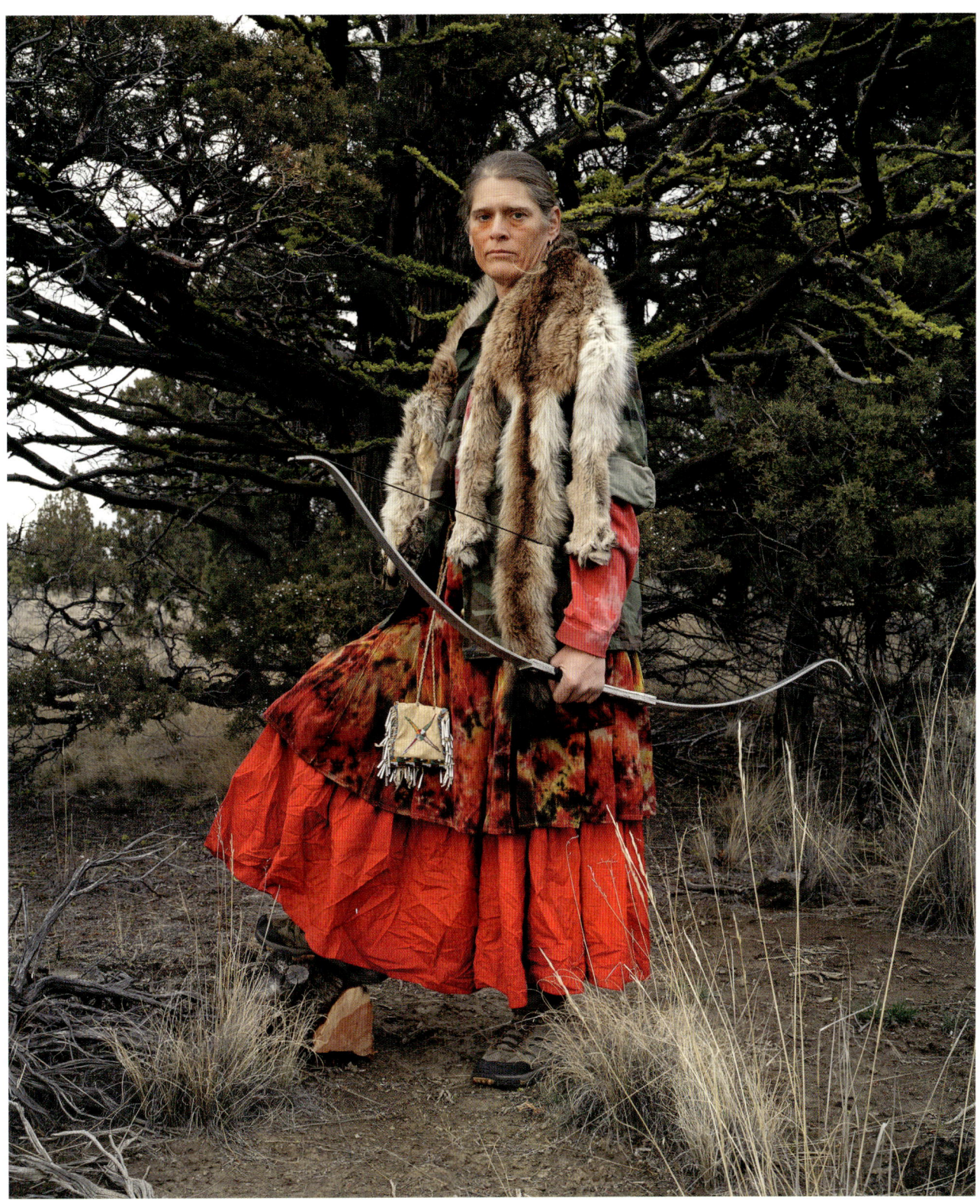

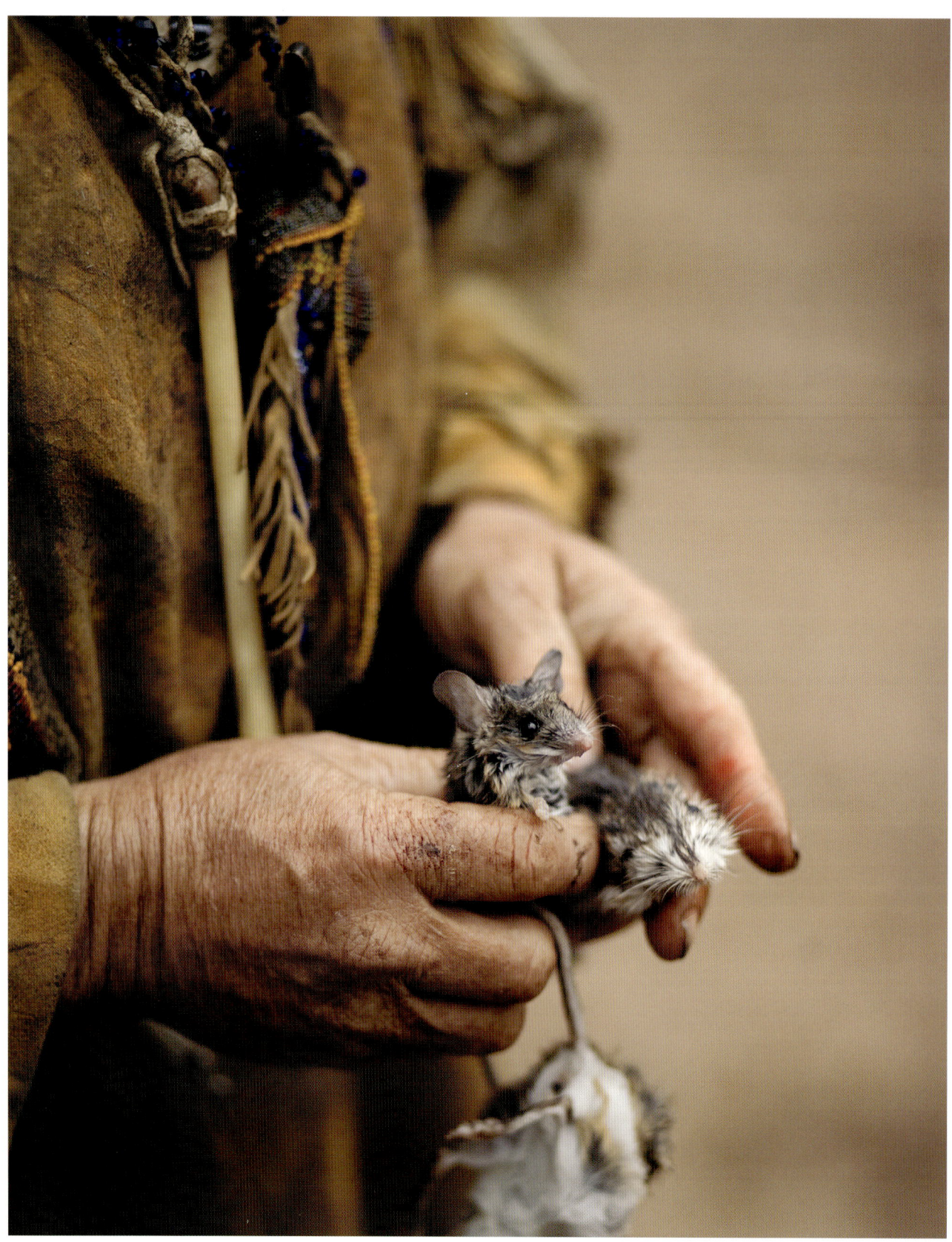

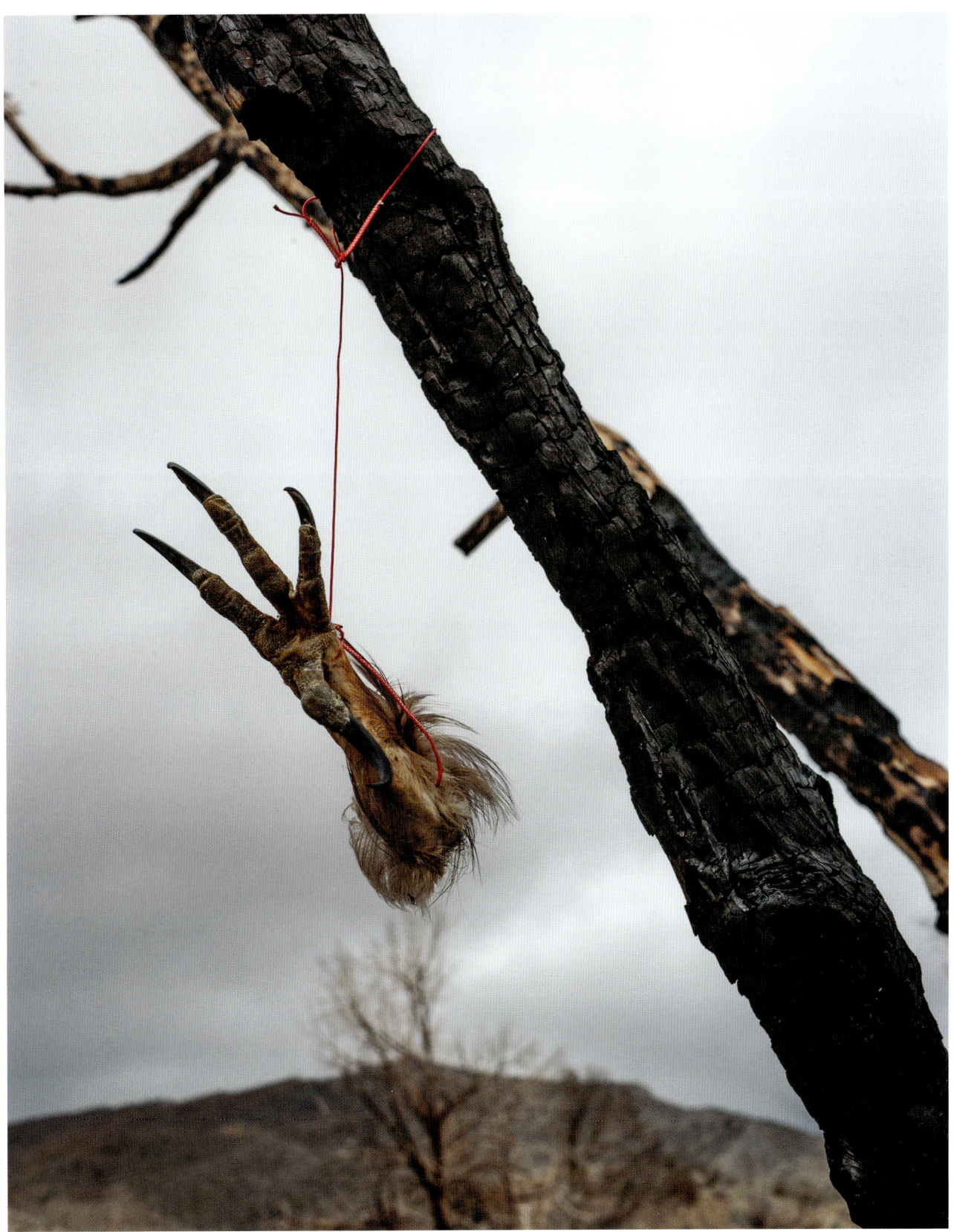

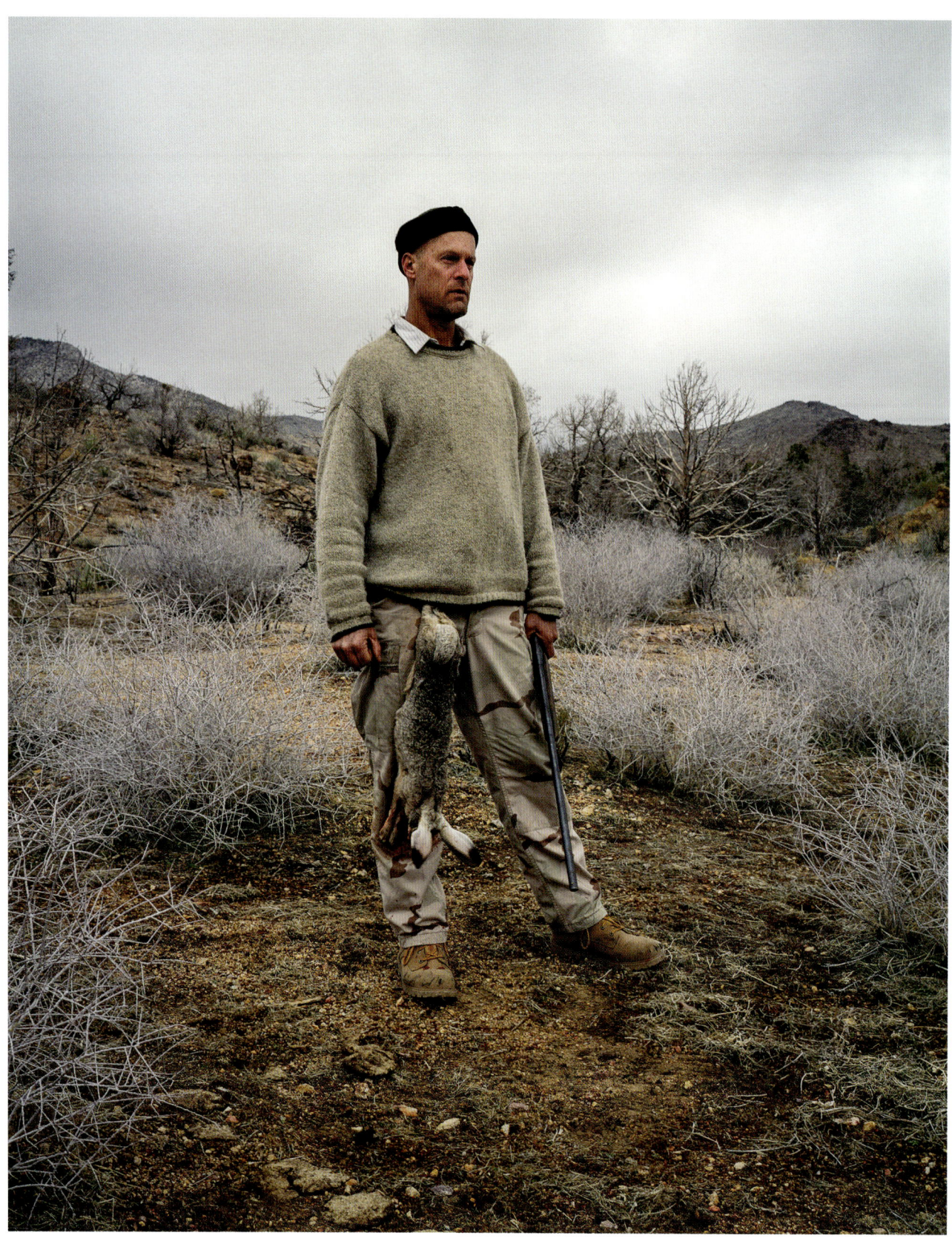

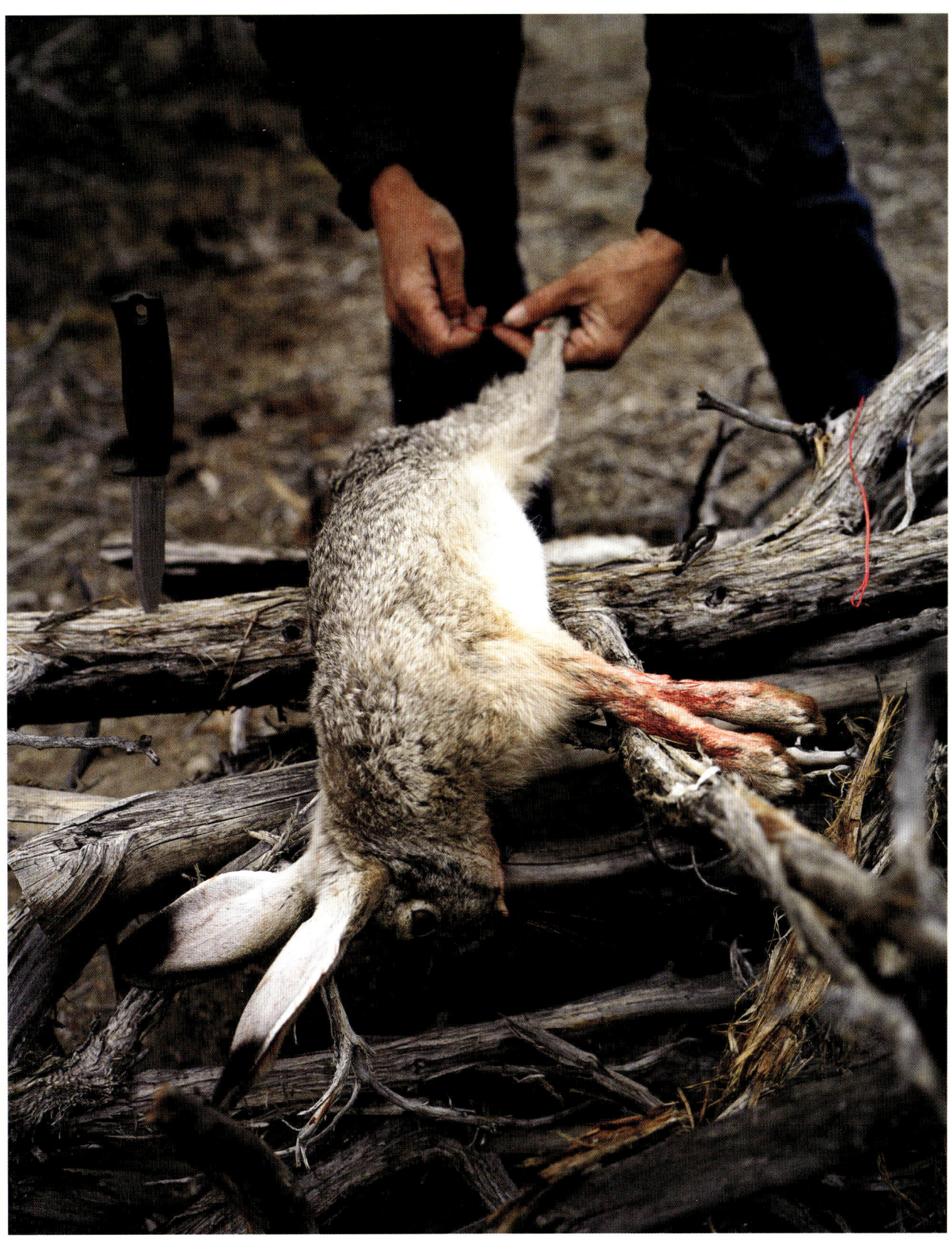

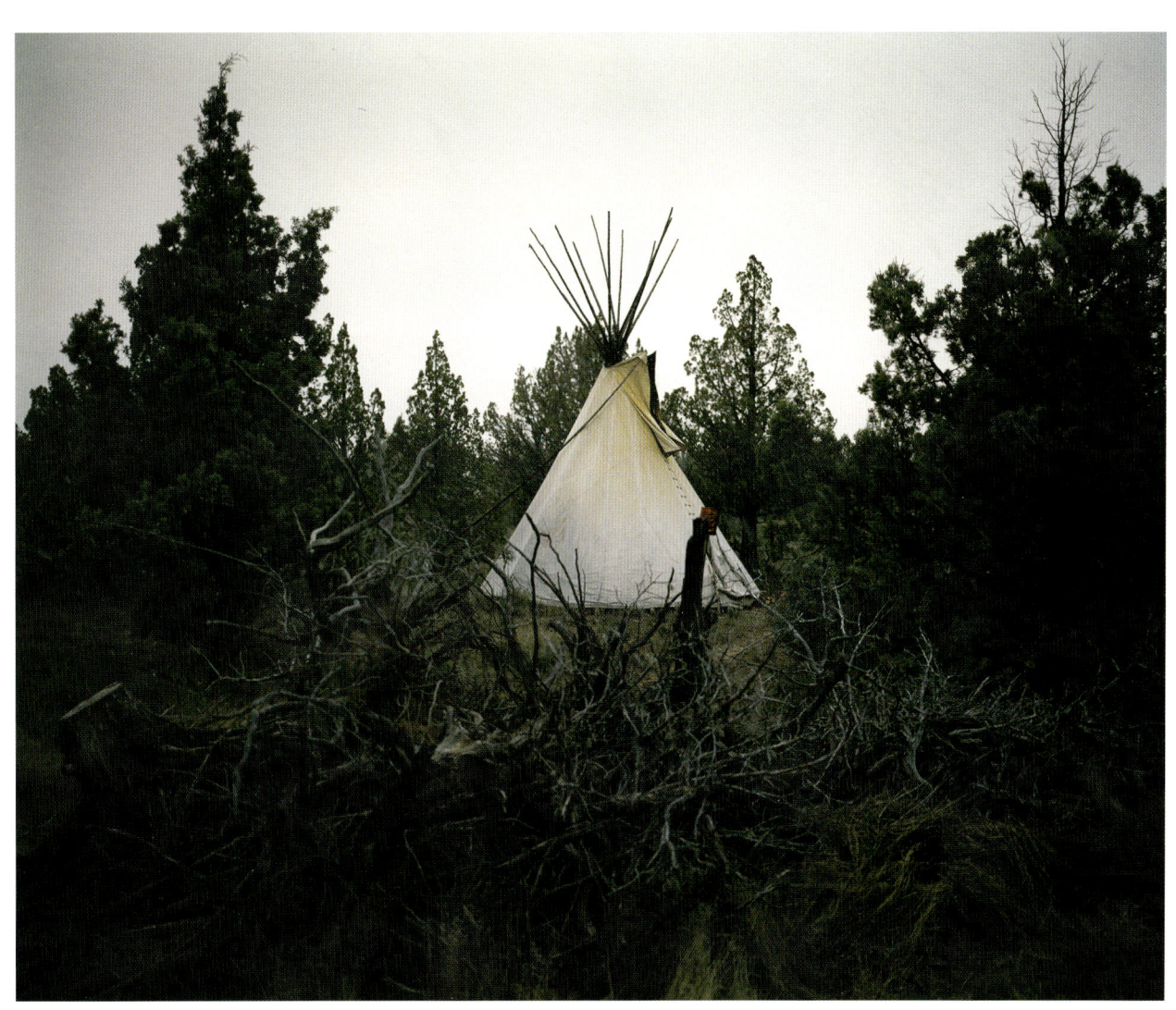

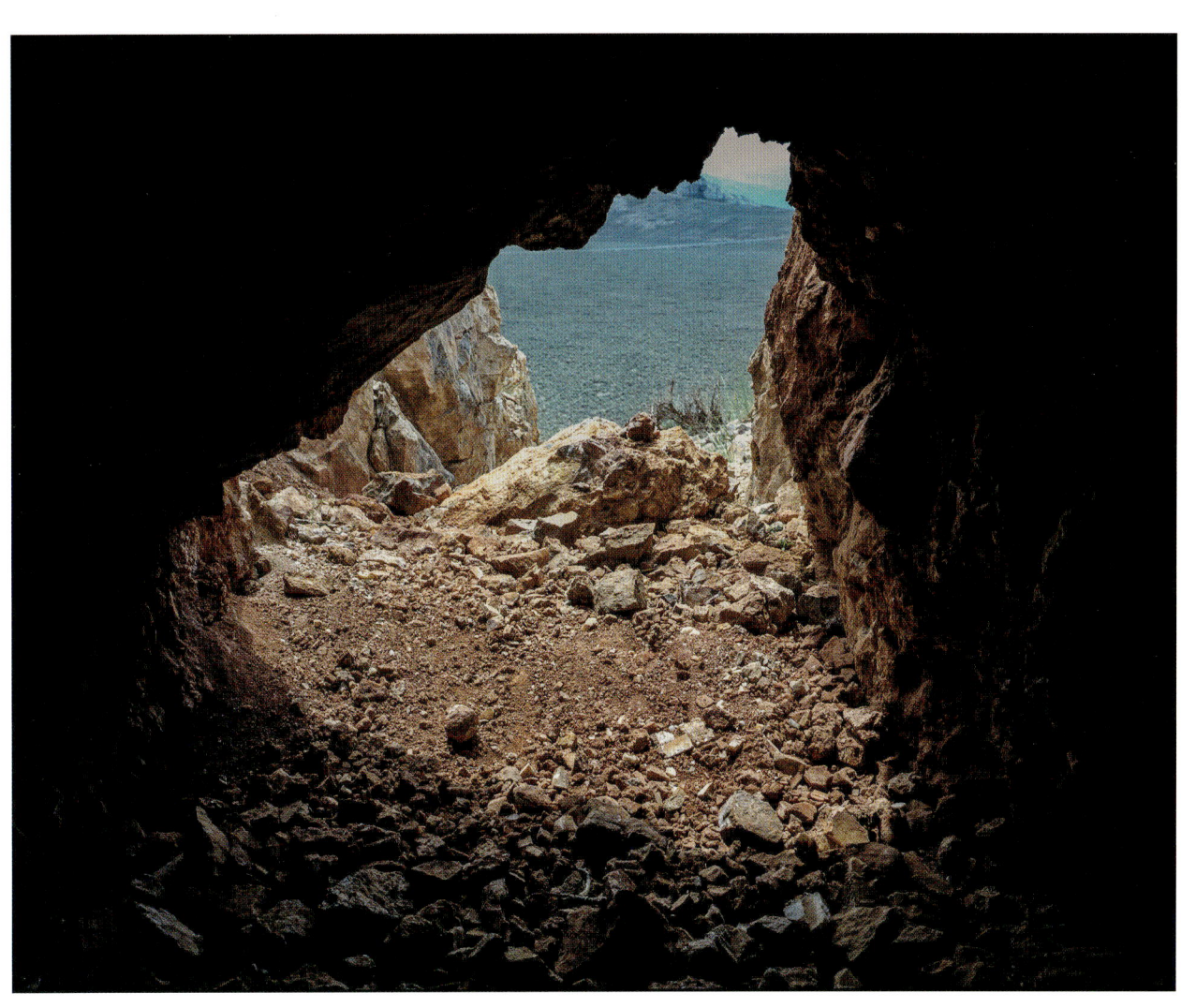

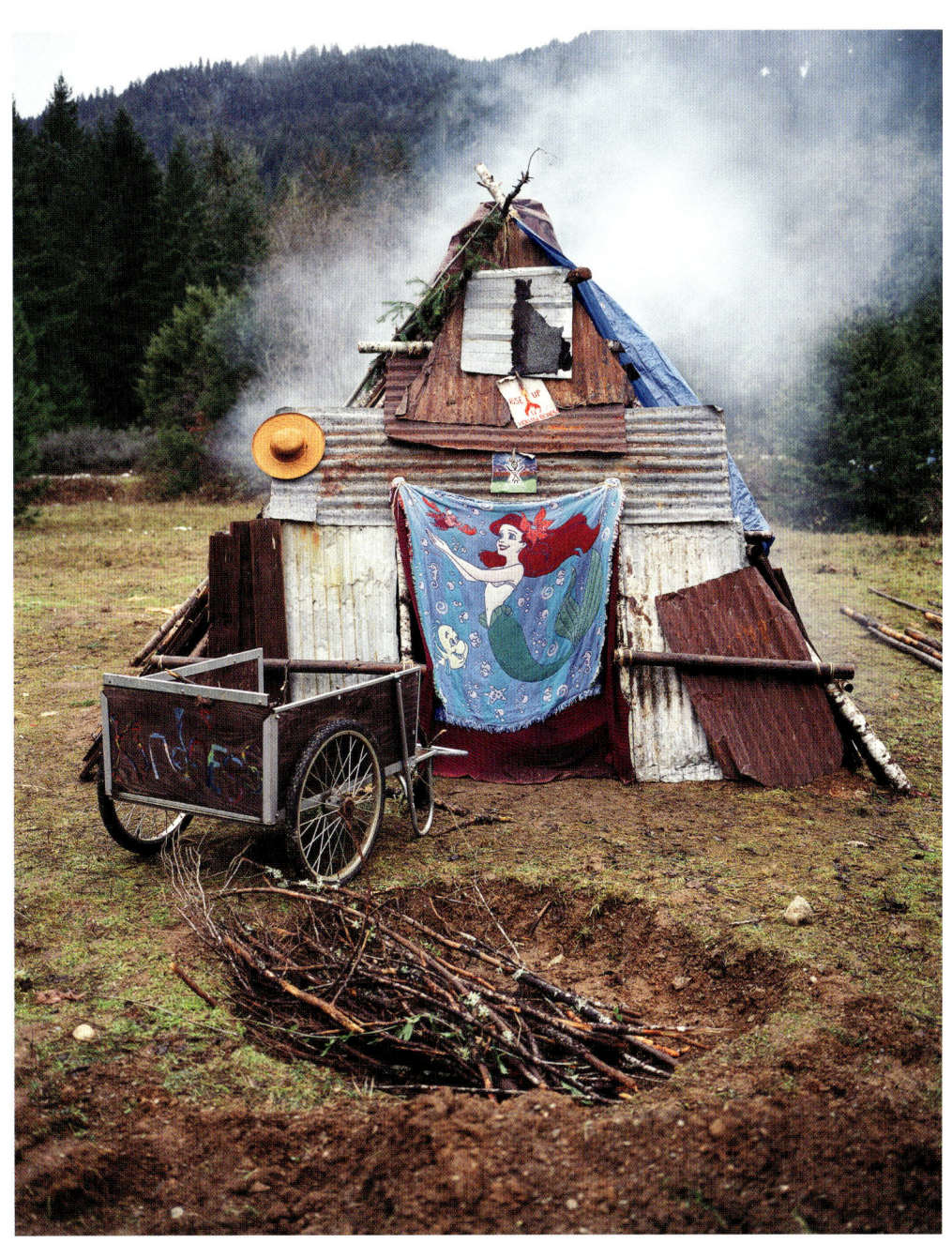

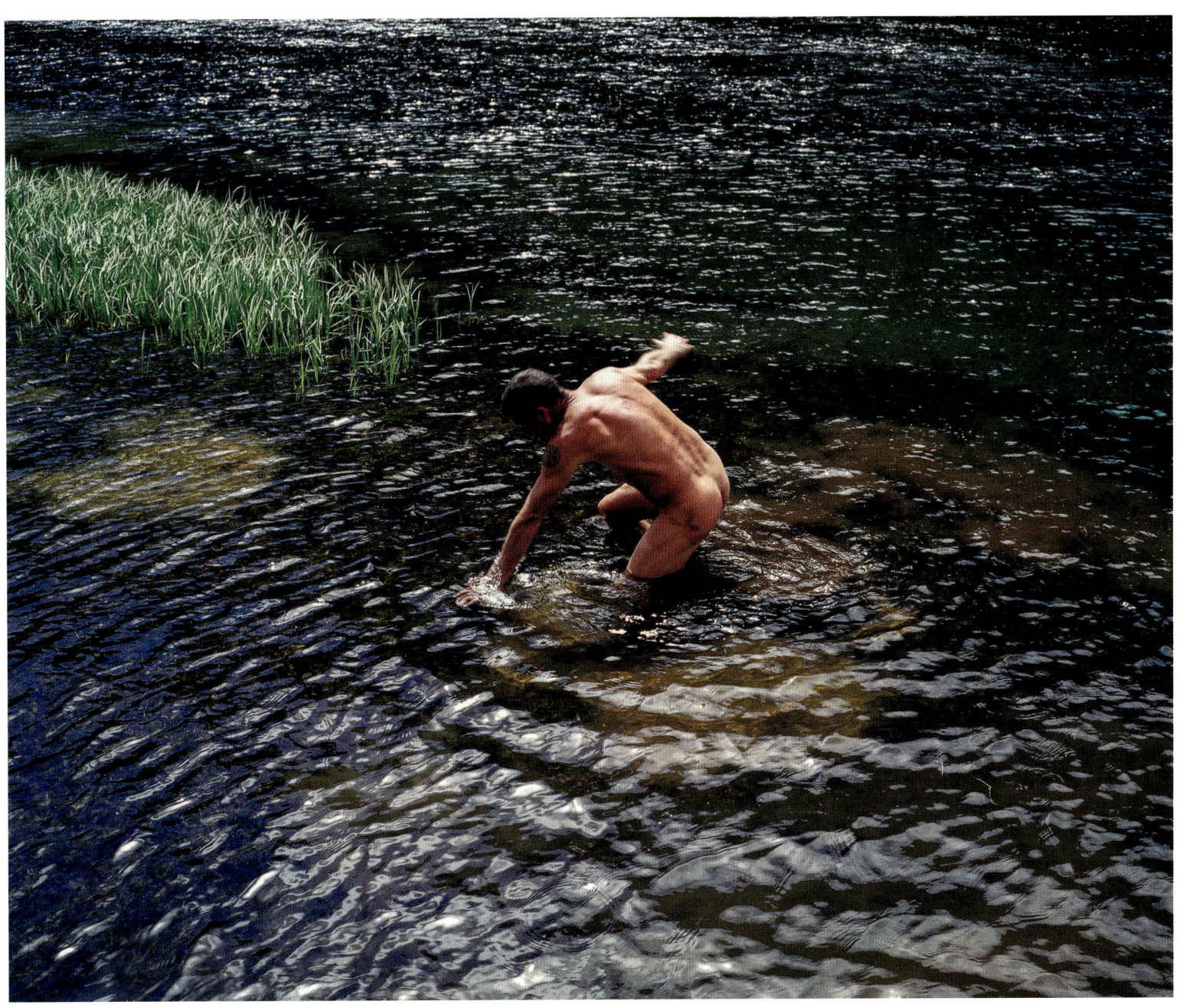

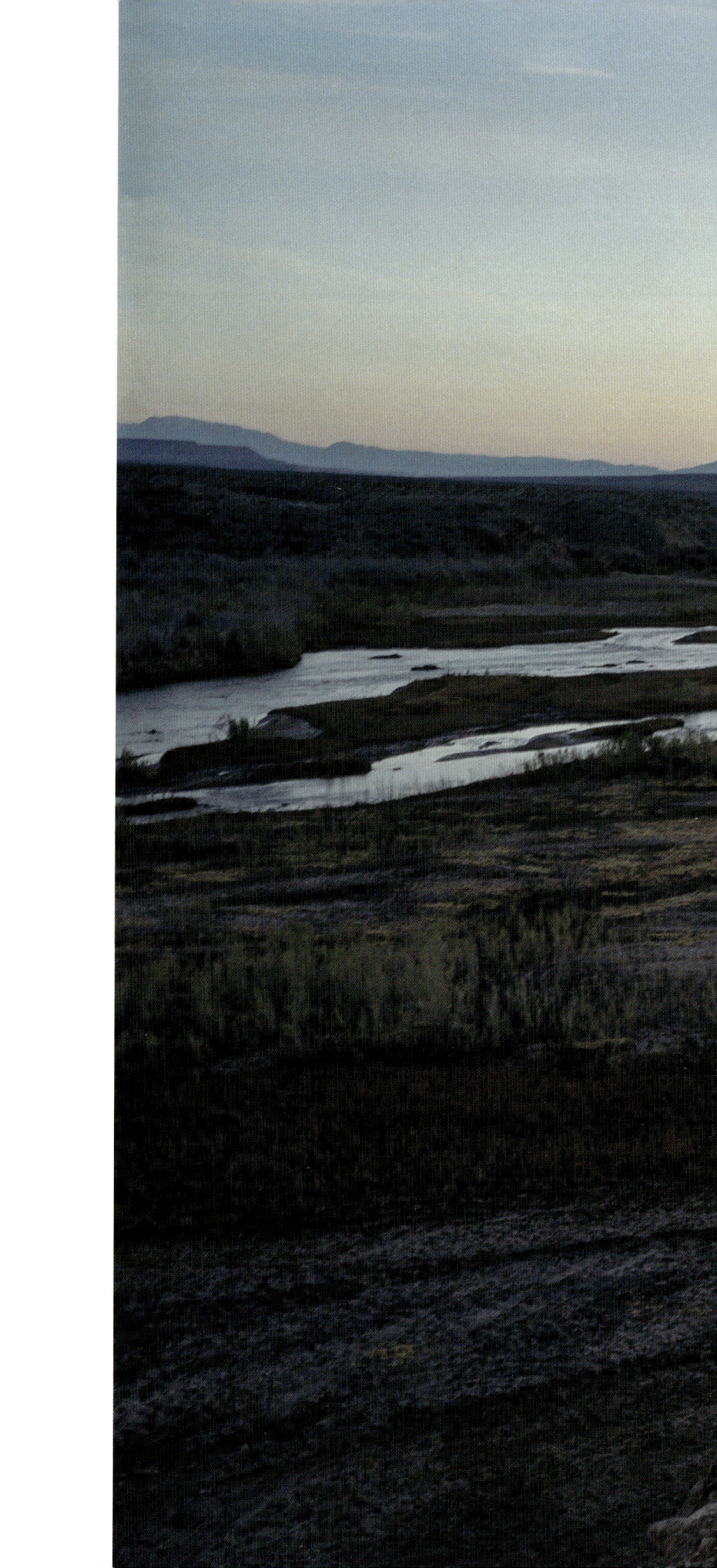

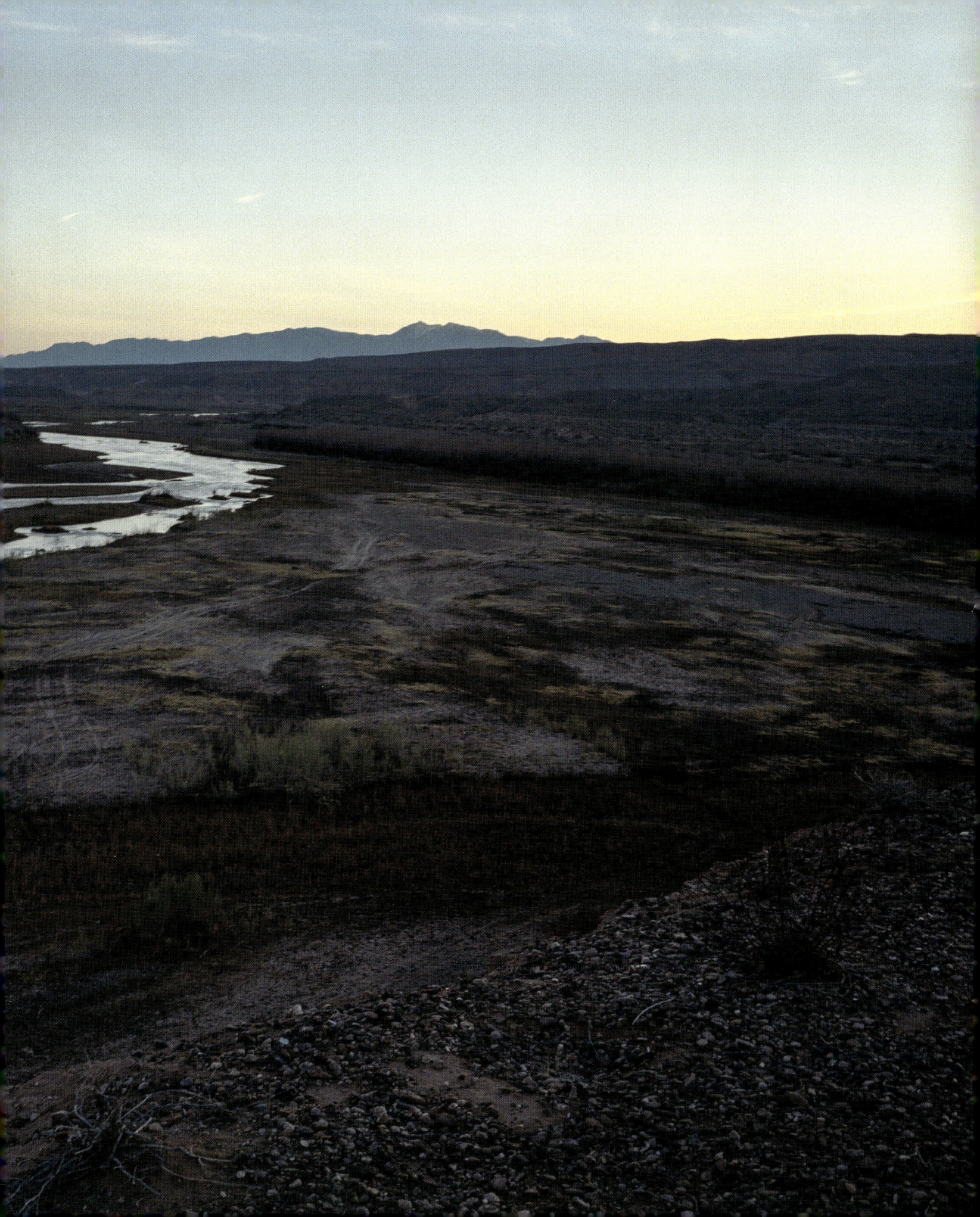

Swim salmon
there's shining salal
in the bright morning sun

Keep swimming salmon
it won't be too long
till the monsters are gone

—JP Hartsong

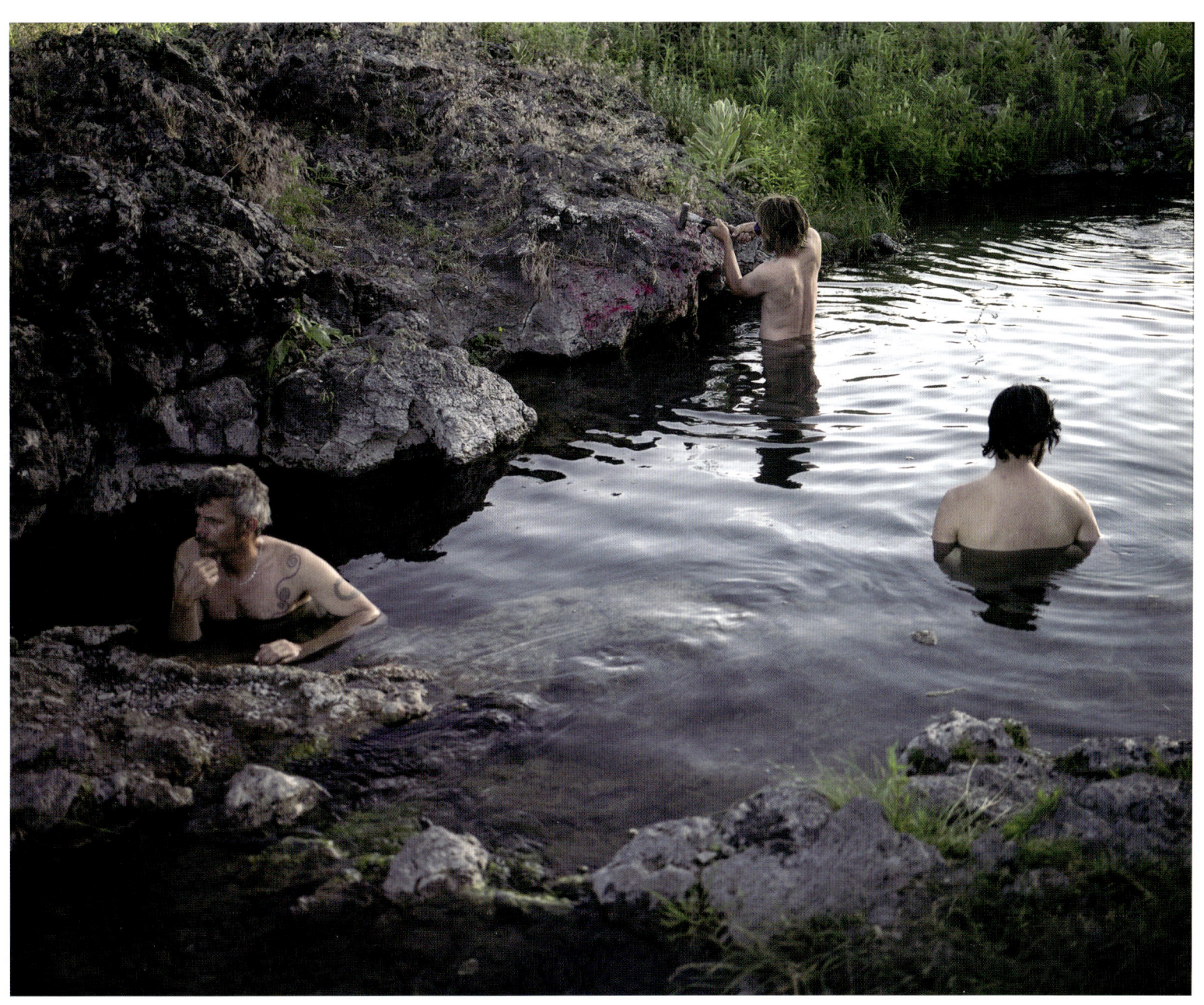

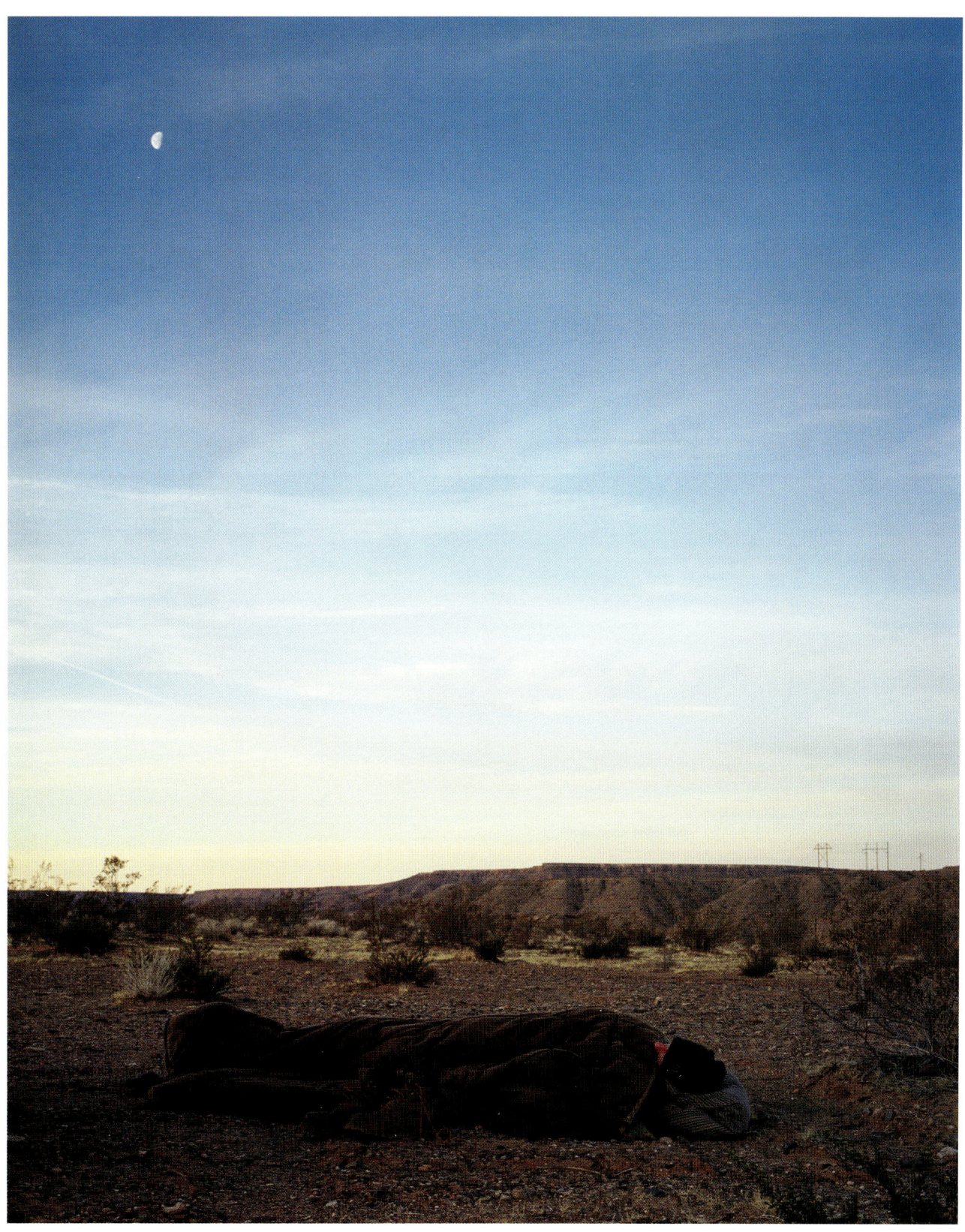

Once there was a wild garden
In the Garden the People were free
and they fed the Garden as they fed themselves

Monster who eats everything
came and one by one
taught the People how to eat BIG
and how to be hungry
the People became so hungry and ate so BIG
they forgot about feeding the Garden

Monster pointed to the west
and the People followed Monster
toward the place of dropping off and dying

They walked and walked and walked
along the way they ate BIG
they were locusts in the field

One by one the People came to the western shore
they looked around
Monster was gone
and it was just the People now

It was dark night
in front of them wave after wave
of dead ocean

Unsure what to do next, one by one
they looked up to Grandmother Moon
and Grandmother Moon said
"Behind the mask is your answer" and she pointed to Blue Star

One by one they turned to see Blue Star
as they stared into the light
they saw the mask and waited

And waited

And waited

Finally the mask opened

Inside the mask one by one
the People saw themselves

They saw themselves eating BIG
they saw themselves
locusts in the field
they saw inside themselves
the Monster who eats everything

And that vision was painful

So painful that one by one
the People fell asleep
because being asleep was easier than seeing

The ancestors came in dreams and whispered
"It's simple, just give back more than you take
you have creation's power in your hands"

And all the People dreamed of planting seeds

Long into the night
one by one
the People began to wake
and for the first time in a very long time
they were not hungry

And one by one they turned to face the east
and one by one they took a step away from
the place of dropping off and dying

Stepping toward the place of new beginnings

Still dark night, they walked cautiously

And one by one they saw the morning star
and one by one they saw the rising sun

The First Nation tribes of indigenous North Americans are most often described as hunter-gatherers, a term which lacks the depth and subtlety, vital to understanding their complex life way.

First Nation People saw every aspect of the world–rocks, plants, animals, wind, fire, people–all as being interconnected, in balance, and everything as being filled with Spirit.

Thus, these First People were bound in duty to consider the whole in their every daily action, and in consideration of the future. Across the continent, there were commonly held ideals like "Plan for the seven generations to come," "Give back more than you take," and "We are all related."

These ideals became indistinguishable from the people's way of life–a way of dynamic and positive interaction with Nature. If you took a plant from the earth, you gave back seeds. If you took an animal, you looked to take the weakest one, leaving the strongest to thrive, thereby strengthening the herd.

Over the millennia, these ways became ingrained in elaborate systems. Digging for roots would, if possible, happen later in the season after the plants had turned to seed. Digging would open a hole in the earth, and seeds were then removed from the plant top and planted back in the hole just dug. If taking roots early in the season, when the plants had no seed, there would be a negative balance. To correct the balance, the people would dig and open thin deep cracks in the earth near thriving plants, cracks where rain would collect, strengthening the existing plants. Months later, the same cracks would receive mature seeds falling from the plants, giving the seeds a better chance to survive.

Set gathering routes were developed by many tribes based on the life cycles of the natural world. The routes would follow seasonal developments and common sense through a variety of terrains, returning at the end of the gathering seasons to a base camp. These routes, circular in nature, developed over generations and became known as Hoops. A typical Hoop would pass through root, berry, and nut terrains, and the people would collect a wide variety of foods, at a time when collection allowed for a positive interaction with the plants. Along the way they would dry and prepare the food for storage. The people would return to base camp prepared for the winter ahead. In the spring the Hoop journey would begin again.

"Give back more than you take" was meant literally. It was both an ideal and a daily practice. The people had known hunger, so "May there be food for seven generations to come" was a sincere daily prayer. "We are all related" referred not only to the people but also to all things. The people were just one part of the whole, and they saw their place humbly.

We gratefully acknowledge and salute the people whose images appear in this book: Amara, Badger, Finisia, JP Hartsong, Jaimie, John, Lauren, Leopard, Lopi, Mikalia, Ray, Skunk, Tate, and Fannie Bird.

We would also like to acknowledge the generous support and encouragement of Tim Wride, WM Hunt, Jim Lurie, Chuck Mobley, Danny Orendorff, Adrienne Skye Roberts, Michelle Dunn Marsh, Mike Roe, Chris Rauschenberg, John Caperton, Murray Edelman, Rory Sparks, and Taj Forer.

For inspiration as well as editorial support with the written text we gratefully acknowledge
Michael Sage Ricci and John Jack Hall.

We offer our humble thanks and deepest appreciation.

With deepest gratitude for all the amazing love and support we recieved for
our Kickstarter campaign we would like to acknowledge:

Aster Max, Pat Johnson and Ferkie, Stella Maris, Norah Morgan, Kaj-anne Pepper, Victoria Carlson, Eric Polito, Catherine Hennessy, Kristen Keith, Steven Miller, Mark Mitchinson, Hollis Melton, Anastasia Green, Johnscott Lee, Rain Crowe, Heidi Lender, Jordan Rockford, Sallie Ann Glassman, Kwai Lam, Kalama Reuter, Liza Bambenek, Scott Walter Snedeker, Willian Hall, Mark Lunetta, Anthony Prud'homme, Essayan Hart, Christopher Rauschenberg, David Thomson, Sarah Huber, Rosalind Solomon, Harry (Solchilde) Rezzemini, Leo Schuman and Michael Henry, David Dunham, Tim B. Wride, Jeff Rose, Blossom Merz, Pablo Colon, Alex Jade, Tony Glore, Eric Nugent, Rebecca Farr, Patrick R. Curry, LRae York, Paul Ellis, Dominic Vine, Stephen Silha, Charles Mantei, Chaliceb, Kent Wright, Danny Orendorff, Deborah Bradford, Doug Bruce, Dan Robinet and Stan Suchan, Julia Miller, Zachary McAdoo, Favero Greenforest, Christopher Rocca and David Rosen, Gloria Babcock, Carol Bennett, WM Hunt, Guy Ambrosino and Kate Winslow, Murray Edelman, Queen Mae Butters, Roran Littleseed, Daniel Torrence and Keith Moree, Jim Westerland, Catherine Ti, Cindy Keith, Michael Sage Rici and Tom Spanbauer, Melissa Thomas Keefer, Joseph Lazaro Rodriguez, Mark Fleming, Gay Block, Carolyn Clark Beedle, Gail Gibson, Joan Morgenstern, Davora Linder, Jeffrey Westphal, Jeffrey Capp, Long Wolf, Jared Morgan, Bema Self Cic, Matthew Ruby, Jonell Kelsey, Heron Saline, Mike Richan, Apple Blossom, Genine Bradwin, Jason, Willem Larsen, Thaddeus Koster, Wes Hurley, Carol Dass, Zee Boudreaux, Jonathan Saruk, Lisa Genuardi Wilson, Gregory J. Zaleski, Trevyn Michaud, Susan Mausshardt, Skybear, Anja Kominicki, Deb Hefford, Amy Wolf, Heather MacEachern, Asrik Tashlin, Sky Nebulah, Vivian Keulards, Aline Smithson, Julie Gant, S. Ruth Gillings, Jesse Bryant, Eric Slade, John Blomgren, Greta Sheldon, Carlton Solle, Susan Craig, Ronald Rognstad, Carolina Duncan, Mr. Tesek, Brian Paul Clamp, Paul Wirhun, Kristiane Koch Riddle, Rachel Venning, Kelli Connell, Cy, Ethan Wright, Alex Moore, Juei-Chen Chao, Greg Rogers, Corinne Hollister, Joslin Van Arsdale, Adam Boehmer, Christopher Corey, Matthew Mollenkopf, Bus No. 8, Jane Smallman, Kayleigh Dance, Chris Willoughby, Mark Lunetta, Dickie Mitchell, Laura, Evelyn Orme, Ariel Shanberg, Robert Baba Sink, Eric Johnson, Jen Hofer, Alejandro Cartagena, Edward George, Linc Madison, Mark Wurth, Bob Schatz, Maria Sparsis, Bobby Dominguez, Josh Klien-Kuhn, Alan WInslow, Ralph McGinnis, Connor Stedman, Julia Vandenoever, Andrew Wood, Fruithurst Wood, Lorien Bales, Hex Agonal, Robert Pennington, Chad States, Monica Roxburgh Jodi Kansagor, Stevee Postman, Deb Przepasniak, Alixandre Long, Pamela Thompson, John Plummer, Jeffry Mitchell, Adrienne Taggart, Ross Taylor, Lizz Randall, Sheilah Wilson, Wolf Martinez, Michael Lecker, Dusty Dmitri Bloomingheart, Helen M. Carothers, Nate Gowdy, Ivan Donovan, Eric Damon Walters, Miguel Mendias, Adam Brown, Mandy Greer, Daniel McInnis, The Silas Finch Foundation, Gayle Sammons, Robert, David Kwasigroh, Ben Neihart, Wendy Young, Moira Brown, Sandor Katz, Frank Yamrus, Michael Philichi, Jennifer McClure, Wash Westmoreland, Frankie Dailey, Richard Kasden, Rodney Rogers, Geroge McClintock, Fernando Quintino, Magdalena Ward, John Brennan, Paula Sjunneson, Jennifer Hawke, Gemma-Rose Turnbull, Jack John Hall, Clyde M Hall, Anne Tucker, Melanie McWhorter.

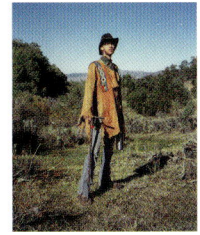

JP Hartsong
Stoneberger Creek, Nevada

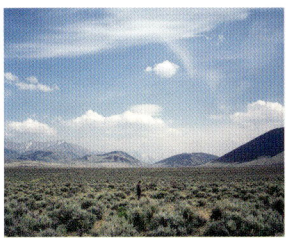

sage field
Lone Pine Ridge, Idaho

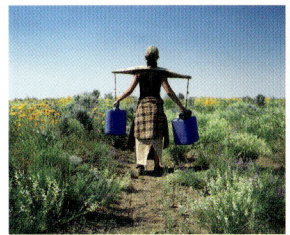

carrying water
Huddles Holes, Craters of
the Moon, Idaho

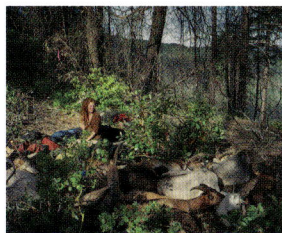

morning
Marble Mountain
Wilderness, California

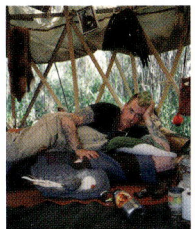

in the wickiup
Arco, Idaho

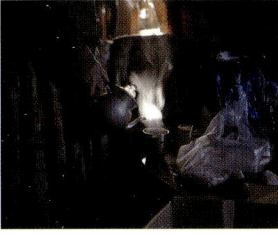

coffee
Arco, Idaho

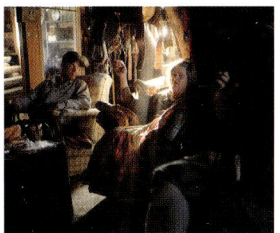

in the cabin
Arco, Idaho

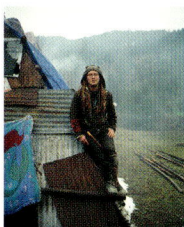

Lopi
Wolf Creek, Oregon

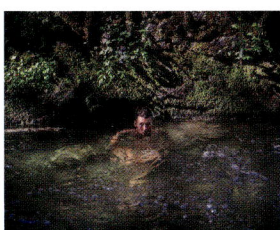

creek
Steinacher Creek, California

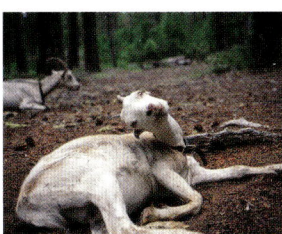

Fannie Bird
Marble Mountain
Wilderness, California

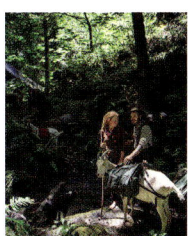

Amara and Ray
Marble Mountain
Wilderness, California

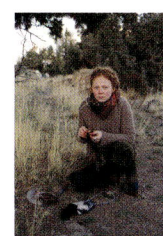

magpie
Deschutes River
Canyon, Oregon

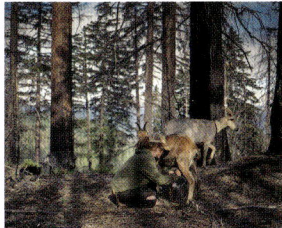

milking
Marble Mountain
Wilderness, California

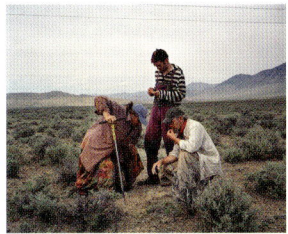

searching
Lone Pine Ridge, Idaho

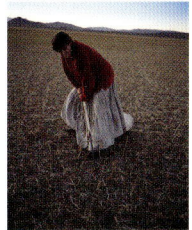

camas prairie
Idaho

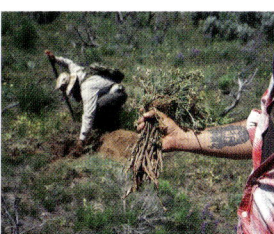

breadroot
Huddles Holes, Craters of
the Moon, Idaho

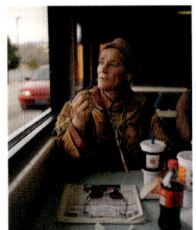

Burger King
Mesquite, Nevada

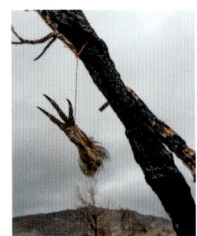

untitled
northeast of
Mormon Peak, Nevada

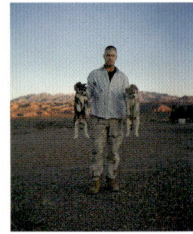

wolf pups
north of
Virgin Peak, Nevada

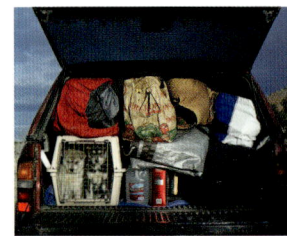

truck
Dodge Pocket, Nevada

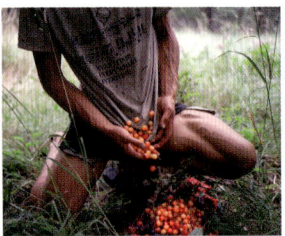

cherries
Marble Mountain
Wilderness, California

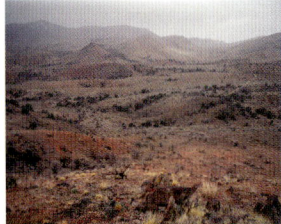

"Dodge Pockets"
Dodge Pocket, Nevada

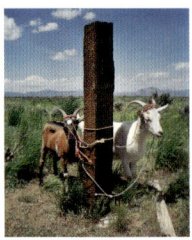

waiting
Huddles Holes, Craters of
the Moon, Idaho

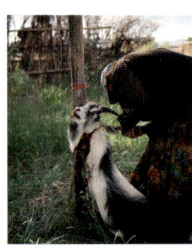

dispatched
Lost River, Idaho

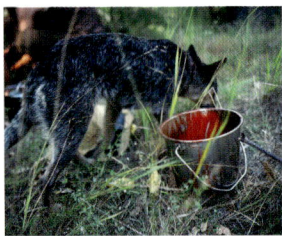

bucket
Steinacher Creek, California

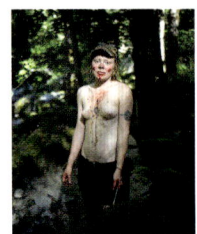

blood makeup
Steinacher Creek, California

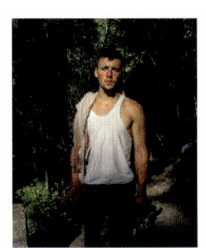

blood moustache
Steinacher Creek, California

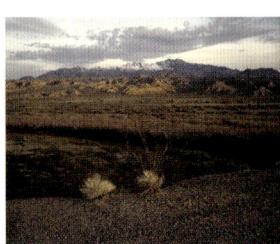

untitled
Nevada

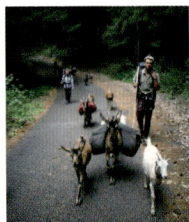

trek
Marble Mountain
Wilderness, California

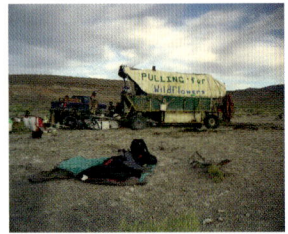

pulling for wildflowers
Spencer Hot Springs,
Nevada

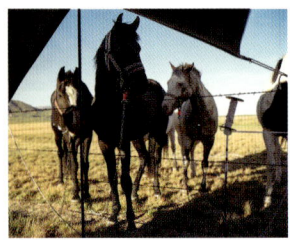

horses
Root Camp, Idaho

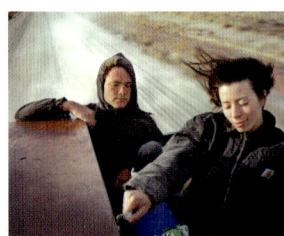

back of the truck
Nevada

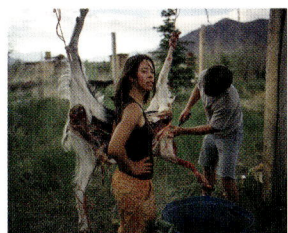

dressing a carcass
Arco, Idaho

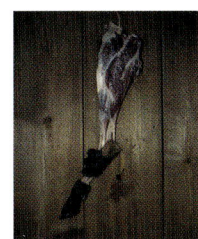

steak with a hoof
Huddles Holes, Craters of
the Moon, Idaho

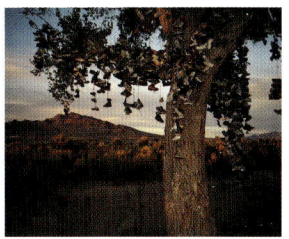

shoe tree
US–50, Nevada

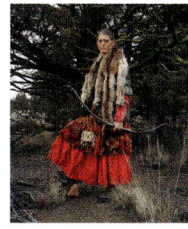

Mikalia
Deschutes River
Canyon, Oregon

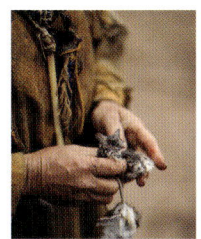

mouse in hand
Dodge Pocket, Nevada

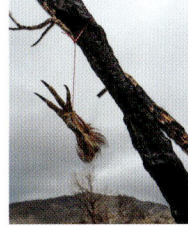

claw
northeast of
Mormon Peak, Nevada

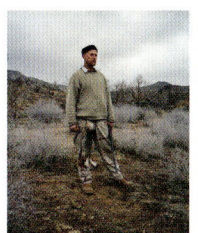

Badger/Bunny
Dodge Pocket, Nevada

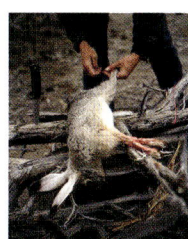

knife
Dodge Pocket, Nevada

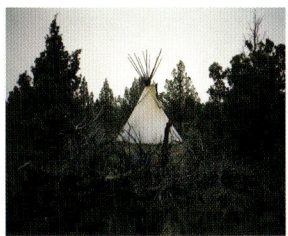

Dirty Skirts
Geneva, Oregon

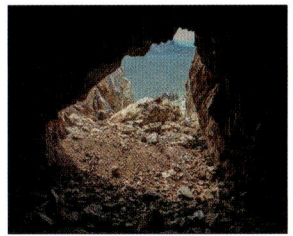

heart of the mother

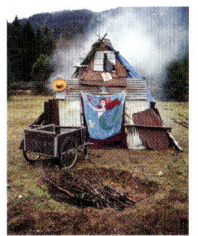

longhouse
Wolf Creek, Oregon

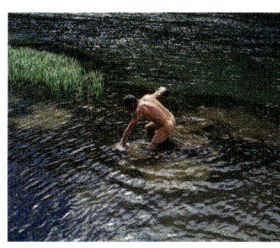

water dance
Deschutes River, Oregon

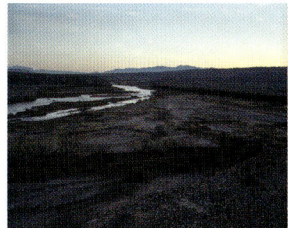

nightfall
Virgin River, Nevada

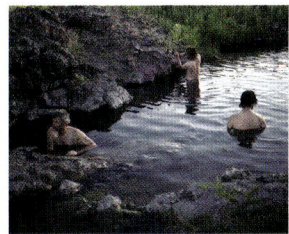

cleaning graffiti off the rock
US–20, Idaho

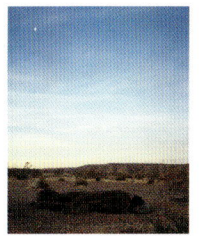

sleeping
east of Las Vegas, Nevada

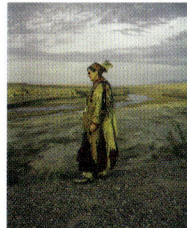

Finisia
The Hoop

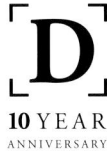

10 Y E A R
ANNIVERSARY

Editors: Taj Forer and Michael Itkoff
Design: Rory Sparks
Copyediting: Michael Sage Ricci

Daylight Books
E-mail: info@daylightbooks.org
Web: www.daylightbooks.org

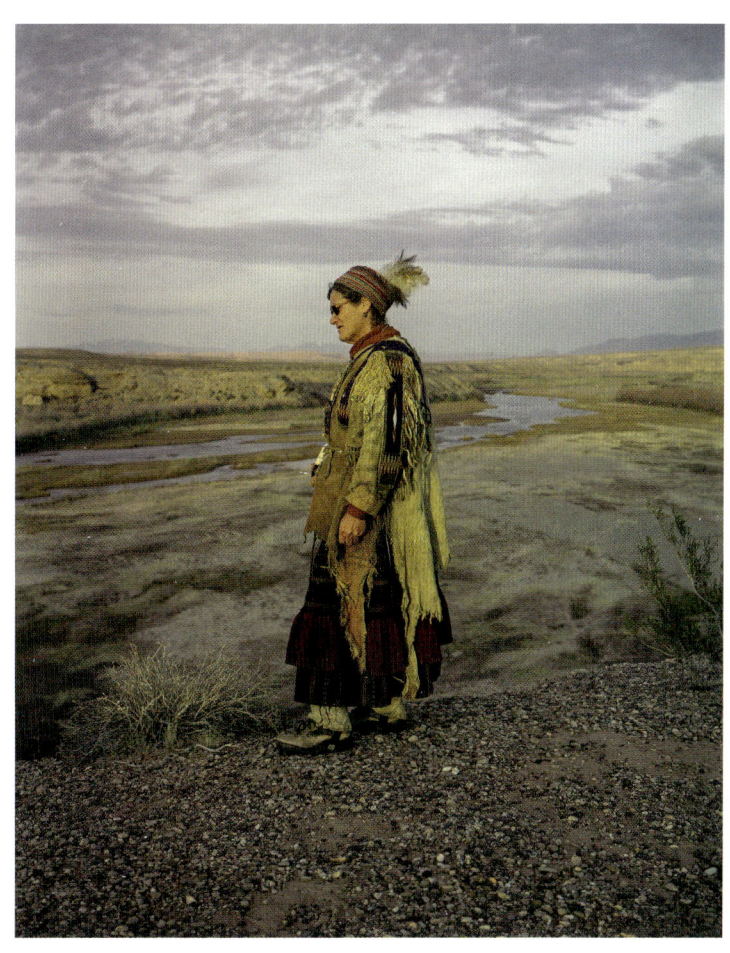